Past Acclaim for Gene Steuerle

Few people have had a greater impact than Gene Steuerle on the major changes in the tax law.

-- Larry Gibbs, former Commissioner of IRS

Great book. I could not put it down…[Dead Men Ruling] addresses a vital concern to those of us who study the gains possible by investing early and well in children

-- James Heckman, Nobel Prize Laureate and professor of economics, University of Chicago.

His definitive and objective history combines sound economic analysis and punctures a few myths.

-- James Tobin, Nobel Laureate, Yale University

Suppose we just got one person to handle the job of reforming Social Security. My nominee for the position of "Social Security Czar" is Gene Steuerle.

-- Andrew Samwick, Professor of Economics, Dartmouth College

A scholar and public servant unmatched in public finance, Eugene Steuerle cogently explains how [entrenched programs] have come to impede economic opportunity and undermine our democracy.

-- Jonathan Cowan, President of Third Way

If we are ever going to break free from the structural deficits weighing down the future, we will need the kind of positive vision Steuerle provides.

-- Robert Bixby, Executive Director, Concord Coalition

Steuerle highlights structural and system changes that will allow us to pursue a new vision [of] investments to combat child poverty, child abuse and neglect, infant mortality and childhood obesity."

-- Bruce Lesley, First Focus (on Children)

"Gene cuts through the gridlock of present arguments to provide a vision for meeting the present and future challenges of governance. This is the most original and thoughtful fiscal policy work in a very long time."

-- Stanford G. Ross, former Social Security Commissioner.

"[A] positive vision for making fiscal policy once again an enabler of economic growth and opportunity."

-- Will Marshall, President, Progressive Policy Institute

I think it fair to say that Treasury I [the Treasury proposal leading to the Tax Reform Act of 1986] would not have moved forward had it not been for [Gene's] early leadership.

-- Ronald A. Pearlman, former Assistant Secretary of the Treasury for Tax Analysis

He makes a compelling case that a nation that does not invest in its children is a nation in decline.

-- Ruby Takanishi, former president of the Foundation for Child Development.

Foreword

Why this book? Why now? Our nation faces a crisis of democracy, but I'm not referring to the one that has occupied voters in recent election campaigns and won't be solved simply whenever Democrats or Republicans win elected office.

Put simply, past presidents and congressional representatives —zombies from the past—have increasingly sought and succeeded in gaining extraordinary control of the future of government action. They have put many obligations, promises, and constraints into the law over how government money will be spent and how taxes can be far below what is necessary to cover those costs. Consequently, today's elected officials have remarkably little ability to adjust the course of government to meet the needs and opportunities of the time.

Things have gotten so out of hand that essentially all the revenues coming into the federal government (and soon much more) have already been committed for all years to come.

This crisis of "fiscal democracy" is coming to a head soon. Signals include Social Security and Medicare shortfalls, rapidly rising government interest costs, the expiration of a recent tax cut that, if extended, threatens even more significant deficits, and little or no preparation for any new crisis. Remember: we've already had three major crises this century and never paid for any of them. Meanwhile, all the political posturing over cultural warfare, debt limits, and government shutdowns reflect a government that fails to do its job.

So, beyond caring about the issue, why dig into this book? I fear that most politicians, even those concerned about the nation's debt, don't understand that traditional budget, spending, and tax reforms can't by themselves solve the democratic issue. They have a quasi-constitutional crisis on their hands. Even at the risk of losing their office, they must understand how we got here. Only then can they break the shackles their predecessors have made on democratic decision-making.

Dedication and Acknowledgements

I dedicate the book to my wife, Marge, for her extraordinary dedication to others, of whom I am lucky enough to be one.

I also wish to acknowledge my great debt to my colleagues, too many to mention, at the Treasury, the Urban-Brookings Tax Policy Center, and the Urban Institute. Much of what I have learned came from interactions with these fabulous people.

Table of Contents

Chapter 1	The Big Mess We're In	1
Chapter 2	We're at a Major Fiscal Crossroads!	12
Chapter 3	Where Did All This Mess Come From?	22
Chapter 4	The Gradual Demise of Fiscal Democracy	31
Chapter 5	From Controlling the Present to Controlling the Future	44
Chapter 6	The Four Deadly Economic Consequences	56
Chapter 7	Three Deadly Political Headaches	67
Chapter 8	The Counterrevolution	78
Chapter 9	Stepping Outside the Hall of Fiscal Mirrors	89
Chapter 10	Restoring Fiscal Freedom and Ending Zombie Rule	98
About the Author		110
Index		112

Chapter 1: The Big Mess We're In (And How We Might Fix It)

If you don't know where you are going, you might wind up someplace else. -- Yogi Berra

Hey there, fellow Americans! Let's discuss the hidden truth in plain sight: how our country's financial situation hinders progress, despite our unprecedented wealth. It's not pretty, folks. We're in an ever-tighter bind, and it's time we recognize the cause and fix the vast damage it's causing.

Remember when America was all about breaking new ground and doing the impossible? From creating the world's first modern democracy to landing on the moon, we've always been a nation of go-getters. But lately? It feels like we've lost our mojo.

These days, we can't do anything without running into huge political hurdles. Whether it's fixing our crumbling roads, giving our children a decent education, or just getting our government to function without constant drama, we're stuck in a rut. Everyone is pointing fingers at our massive budget deficits.

Now, don't get me wrong—those deficits are a problem. Our national debt has skyrocketed to $34 trillion as of 2024. That's a lot of zeroes. But here's the thing: deficits are only a symptom of a much bigger issue.

Beyond Zombie Rule

The Real Problem: We're Trapped by the Past

So, what's really going on? Over the last few decades, both Democrats and Republicans have been playing a game of "let's control the future."

Down and Out Uncle Sam

They've created a bunch of programs that automatically grow faster than a teenager in a growth spurt, eating up every extra dollar the government takes in each year. At the same time, they've locked in tax cuts that leave Uncle Sam increasingly unable to pay his current bills.

The result? These parties have effectively conspired to put us in a fiscal straitjacket. Today's politicians and voters have very little wiggle room or fiscal freedom to choose their priorities or tackle new challenges. We're basically stuck maintaining yesterday's pet projects, paying ever less of their cost, and leaving the bills to future taxpayers.

Let me break it down for you:

1. On the spending side, we've got these things called "mandatory spending," mainly "entitlements," like Social Security, Medicare, and Medicaid. They accomplished a lot

of good, but for decades they've grown automatically, year after year, faster than the economy itself. And they are scheduled to do so essentially forever. No matter what new needs pop up, these programs keep demanding more and more of the budget pie.

2. On the tax side, we've slashed rates and maintained many deductions and credits that grow automatically. The result? The government is taking in way less money than it needs to pay for all the stuff we've promised ourselves.

We have an endless buffet, but we only charge for salad. Something's got to give, right?

The Fiscal Democracy Index: A Scary Reality Check

To show just how bad things have gotten, Tim Roeper and I came up with something called the "fiscal democracy index." It measures how much of our future tax money remains after paying for permanent and usually growing commitments to existing programs and interest on the debt. This index showed that Congress could appropriate over 60% of receipts for most of the 1960s even without running a deficit.

Beyond Zombie Rule

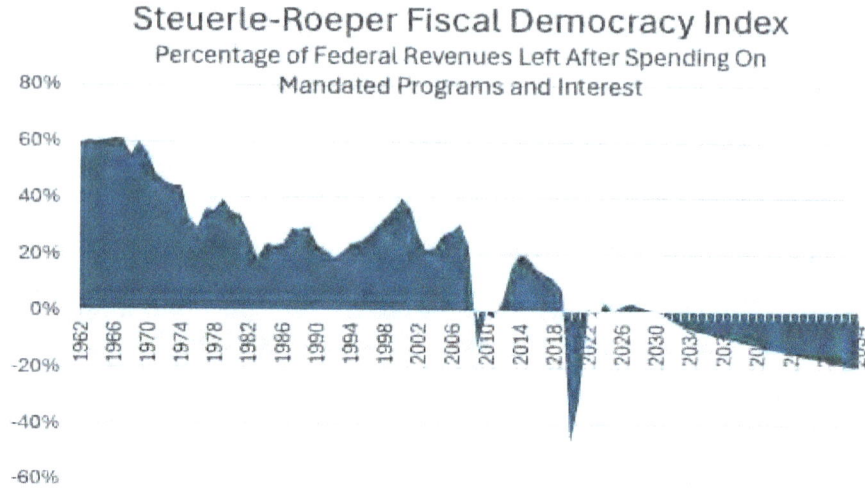

Here's the scary part: In 2009, this index dipped into negative territory for the first time. But at least that was during the worst recession in modern times. And guess what? Unless significant reform occurs, we're moved increasingly into that negative territory, even in the best of times. This implies that the government has already committed more than every single dollar of revenue before each new Congress takes office.

Even if we slashed all the "discretionary" spending—you know, how Congress appropriates things, like education, transportation, and defense—to zero, it wouldn't fix the problem. All these automatically expanding "mandatory" programs would still leave us in chaos. In addition to the ever-increasing debt, the government has also scheduled interest on the debt to increase at a rate faster than a growing economy increases government revenues.

We're telling our kids and grandkids, "Sorry, we spent all the money on ourselves. Good luck figuring out how to pay for schools, roads, and whatever new challenges you'll face!"

How Did We Get Here?

Now, you might wonder, " How did we end up in this mess?" It's a classic case of noble intentions gone wrong.

Today, more than every single dollar of government revenue is already committed before each new Congress even shows up for work.

Both parties like to provide economic certainty and security for people. Democrats focus on issues like poverty and inequality, creating programs to help with retirement, healthcare, and education. Republicans worry about government size and want to keep taxes low to encourage work and savings.

Each of these goals sounds pretty reasonable, right? We went overboard, which is the problem. We tilted so far toward guaranteeing future benefit growth in specific programs and low taxes that we've left ourselves with no flexibility to deal with new challenges.

Beyond Zombie Rule

We're driving a car with the steering wheel locked in place. Sure, we know where we're going, but what happens when we need to avoid an obstacle or take a new road?

The Consequences: A Government Stuck in the Past

So what does this actually mean? Despite our increased wealth, our government continues to remain stagnant, unable to adjust to the evolving world.

Think about it: We created Social Security in 1935, Medicare and Medicaid in 1965, when a large share of the population was uninsured for either retirement or healthcare. The world has changed more than a bit since then, don't you think? We're living longer, having fewer children, facing global competition, and dealing with technological disruptions that would've seemed like science fiction back then.

But our budget? It's still largely focused on putting ever larger shares of our national income onto the priorities of the past. It's like we're trying to navigate the internet age with a budget designed for the Gutenberg Press.

Both parties are guilty here. Liberals want not just to protect but continually expand the same social programs built on the same platforms created decades ago, even if that means soon giving multi-million-dollar retirement packages to well-off seniors while many working families struggle. Conservatives, in turn, are dead set on keeping taxes low, even if it means we can't pay our bills or invest in the future.

Meanwhile, younger Americans are tuning out of politics altogether. Can you blame them? It feels like the grownups are too busy arguing over who is entitled to bigger pieces of a pie to notice the kitchen is on fire.

The Deficit Distraction

You might wonder, "Haven't we tried to fix this before? What about all those deficit reduction efforts?"

You're right; we have tried to face at least some near-term consequences. In fact, between 1982 and 1997, we had five significant deficit-reduction agreements, plus one partial but still major reform to Social Security. We even balanced the budget for four years, from 1998 to 2001.

> **Our budget? It's still largely focused on the priorities of the past.**

But here's the catch: while those efforts helped avoid more immediate crises, they didn't solve the underlying problem. The automatically growing programs kept growing, tax burdens were cut, no money was set aside to pay for the types of crises that occurred, and our fiscal freedom kept shrinking.

It's like we were treating the symptoms without curing the disease. And now, we're sicker than ever.

Beyond Zombie Rule

A Vision for the Future

Alright, enough doom and gloom. Let's talk about what we could do if we fixed this mess.

Imagine a world where, as our economy grows most years, we actually have some extra money to work with. Imagine a scenario where our elected leaders can examine the current issues and take appropriate action. Yes, we can also return that money to the taxpayers.

We're the richest nation in history for crying out loud! We absolutely have the resources to tackle things like job creation, poverty, and investing in our young people. We just need to free up those resources from the death grip of past commitments.

Government spends and provides tax subsidies of over $80,000 per household at all levels (federal, state, and local). That's a lot of dough!

Even with below-average economic growth, we're talking about trillions of dollars more in personal income over the next few years. Within a decade, that could mean over $1 trillion in additional annual revenues for the government, even if tax rates fall a bit.

The possibilities are mind-boggling if we can break free from this fiscal straitjacket that binds all future citizens and their elected representatives to the dictates of dead men (and, yes, they were mainly men).

Beyond Zombie Rule

So, What Do We Do?

Alright, here's the trillion-dollar question: How do we fix this mess?

First things first, we need to realize that just cutting the deficit isn't enough. We need a more fundamental reform—a "big fix," if you will.

At its core, this is what a new set of fiscal rules will require:

1. Democrats agree to limit the eternal automatic growth of any spending program. No more blank checks for healthcare and retirement programs that grow faster than the economy. They'll still grow but through future choices as to priorities.

Political Parties Playing Together

2. Republicans agree to generate enough revenue to pay our bills instead of passing them on to future generations. Limiting ever-growing tax subsidies is also necessary. We should stop assuming that tax cuts are a freebie.

3. Both parties agree to make the budget process more transparent and flexible. They must stop hiding behind

Beyond Zombie Rule

complicated accounting, pretending that money grows on trees or in Fort Knox vaults, and start making real choices.

The goal isn't to dismantle the social safety net or jack up taxes to insane levels. It's to restore some balance and give future generations greater power to make their own choices.

Imagine a government that can actually respond to new challenges and opportunities. A government that can invest in education, infrastructure, and innovation without bankrupting itself. A government that works for the people of today and tomorrow, not just the ghosts of policies past.

It will be challenging. We're asking people to give up some guarantees they've come to expect. However, the alternative—a future where our past commitments impede our ability to tackle new challenges—is significantly worse.

In summary, as we head into second quarter of the 21st century, we're facing all sorts of uncertainty and a whole new set of challenges, including climate change, COVID-19, AI and automation, the Gig economy, and rising healthcare costs.

These challenges are beyond the capabilities of our current budget setup. We need the flexibility to shift resources, try new approaches, and invest in our future.

Beyond Zombie Rule

We can't achieve those goals without facing the facts. Both major political parties have contributed to creating a "fiscal straitjacket" through automatically growing entitlement programs and locked-in tax cuts. The "fiscal democracy index" demonstrates that we've already committed all future tax revenues to ongoing programs. This makes it very difficult to do anything new or even necessary. A "big fix" requires three steps: limiting automatic program growth; generating sufficient revenue to pay our bills currently, at least in good times; and making the budget process more transparent and flexible.

In the next chapter, we'll explore historical parallels to our current situation, looking at two other moments in American history when the nation faced similar fiscal crossroads. Understanding how our ancestors dealt with their fiscal turning points gives us insight into how we might tackle our modern challenges.

Chapter 2: We're at a Major Fiscal Crossroads! We've Been Here Before

Don't fight the problem. Decide it. -- General George C. Marshall

Let's talk about fiscal policy, which, in simple terms, is about figuring out what the government should do and how to pay for it. In formulating that policy, the government cannot ignore, even if it pretends to, all the new political, economic, and social issues that pop up. As our country grows and changes, the folks in charge also need to adapt our programs so we can tackle new problems head-on.

Sometimes, though, more than a bit of tweaking is required for how the government handles its money. That's when we hit what I call a "fiscal turning point"—a moment when we need to overhaul how our government operates. Indeed, we are currently experiencing such a moment.

You can see the signs everywhere. Congress has reached a deadlock; partisanship has surged, cultural warfare has supplanted actual policymaking, and sporadic implementation of arbitrary budget cuts, known as sequesters, has resulted in chaos and provided no solutions. Young people are getting fed up with both major political parties, and some politicians threaten to shut down the government every year. We need to change not just our economic and social policies, but the whole way our government works.

This isn't the first time America's been at a crossroads like this. We've had to make big fiscal changes before, especially at the beginning and end of major wars. But what's really interesting are the times when our old ways of doing things just don't cut it anymore, even without a war forcing our hand.

Two examples stand out. First, there was the early post-Revolutionary period. The government set up under the Articles of Confederation was weak sauce, so our founding fathers had to write a whole new Constitution to create a stronger government. However, the new Constitution left open to democratic decision-making what would be a viable tax or debt policy, the absence of which posed a threat to domestic tranquility and international commerce, jeopardizing our bold democratic experiment. Then, during the Progressive Era, we had to beef up our government to adjust to the new industrial economy and compete with rising powers abroad and big industrialists at home.

To understand how these past turning points relate to what we're dealing with now, let's consider the federal budget differently. Instead of just taxes and spending, let's talk about "giveaways" and "takeaways." Giveaways are the good stuff—tax cuts and spending increases that often benefit specific groups and sometimes everyone. Takeaways are the not-so-fun part—tax hikes or spending cuts that hurt some folks but pay for the giveaways.

Beyond Zombie Rule

Politicians love playing Santa Claus, handing out giveaways to make voters happy and get re-elected. They're not so keen on enacting takeaways that tick people off and cause them to lose elections. This is true everywhere democracy exists—it's just how the game is played. What makes those

earlier turning points relevant is that, like today, they forced politicians to create new systems that involved some large takeaways. People weren't thrilled about it, and many politicians lost their jobs. This reluctance to act resulted in a prolonged worsening of the situation. Sound familiar? We're facing the same kind of challenges today.

Let's take a quick trip back in time to see how our ancestors dealt with these fiscal turning points.

The Post-Revolution Fiscal Fiasco

After the Revolutionary War, America was in rough financial shape. We had to borrow a lot of money from France to fight the war, and even then, we failed to pay our soldiers their due. The situation escalated to such a degree that a group of officers almost marched on the capital to demand their back pay and pensions. It took George Washington to calm them down.

Politicians love playing Santa Claus, handing out giveaways.

Under the Articles of Confederation, we couldn't handle the needs of a growing country. To pay off state and other war debts, taxes needed to be higher than the British taxes against which we rebelled. However, the national government under the Articles couldn't impose taxes, and the states weren't willing or able to cough up the necessary cash.

People were so angry that armed rebellions broke out. Shays' Rebellion was so serious a threat that George Washington had to come out of retirement to help get things under control. But these tax revolts helped convince people that we needed a stronger national government. That led to a new Constitution, but, hey, who wants to take the lead in imposing the taxes authorized by the new government?

Beyond Zombie Rule

Enter Alexander Hamilton, our first Treasury Secretary. This guy had a plan to pay off all of our foreign and domestic debts and take on the states' debts. Honestly, he was pretty good with smoke and mirrors, too. It was a bold move that not everyone loved, especially the Southern states, which had less debt than the Northern states. Though later claiming to be "duped" by Hamilton, Thomas Jefferson would accept his offer to move the capital to Washington, DC, as a compensating compromise. And we think the compromises required today are huge!

Hamilton's plan included several significant changes: more federal borrowing powers, a major federal government revenue source in the form of tariffs, and a more robust Treasury Department. He turned government debt into a legitimate part of the money supply and invested the merchant class in the success of the new federal government.

Will we learn from our history and make choices that set us on a better course?. Or muddle along.

These changes weren't without cost. The new tariffs protected Northeastern manufacturers at the expense of Southerners and Westerners. This power shift eventually led to the decline of the Federalist Party. But despite the political fallout, these fiscal reforms gave the government the power and resources it needed to grow and help the country develop.

The Progressive Era: Dealing with the Industrial Revolution

Enter the Progressive Era almost a century later, led by presidents like Teddy Roosevelt. When Roosevelt left for Africa after his presidency, industrial big shot J.P. Morgan reportedly toasted, "America expects every lion to do its duty!"

The federal government faced pressure to protect workers, help businesses compete, and establish America as a world power. These were national issues that required a more robust federal response.

Again, there were budget crises. In 1897, federal debt skyrocketed due to a poor economy, expensive Civil War pensions, and increased spending on public improvements. The government had tried to raise revenue by hiking tariffs to extremely high rates, but this backfired, hurting consumers and making it harder for American companies to sell goods abroad.

The big changes? Significant developments included introducing a federal income tax, establishing the Federal Reserve for financial management, and implementing new regulations aimed at reining large corporations, especially monopolies. Getting these changes wasn't easy. The individual income tax was especially controversial. The Supreme Court initially said, "No way!" so Congress had to pass a constitutional amendment. It took until 1913 to make it happen. Imagine waiting that long for a software update!

Let's fast-forward to today. We're facing our own fiscal turning point, and it's a doozy.

Beyond Zombie Rule

The Modern Fiscal Mess

Here we are in the middle of the third decade of the 21st century, and do we have some challenges! We're dealing with the aftermath of a global pandemic, dictators are trying to unite against democratic countries, and wage and wealth inequality is off the charts. Since 1980, our national debt has quadrupled as a share of our national income, and it is now roughly equal to our national income. At the end of World War II, the only other time we had debt at this share of national income, revenues were scheduled to exceed spending substantially. Today, laws on the books schedule spending to exceed revenues substantially, swelling deficits even in periods of low unemployment, even without Congress legislating any new giveaway.

Like in those earlier turning points, our current system isn't cutting it. We've got outdated tax codes that aren't keeping up with the digital economy, a Social Security system that's struggling to support an aging population, a healthcare system that eats up more of our budget and national income every year than almost any nation on earth, and rapidly rising interest costs.

Uncle Sam Hitting the Gym

And let's not forget the political gridlock. Congress can barely agree on a

Beyond Zombie Rule

budget, let alone make the significant changes we need. We've had government shutdowns, debt ceiling standoffs, and a lot of finger-pointing.

But here's the thing—we've been here before and found ways to adapt and overcome. We need the same bold thinking and willingness to make tough choices that our ancestors showed during previous fiscal turning points.

Whatever the details—and we'll get into more detail in later chapters—one thing is clear: we need to be able to choose without being beholden to laws written by now-dead legislators, controlling the Congress and the President like Zombies rising up to threaten electoral defeat for anyone trying to do the right thing. As Hamilton and the Progressives did, we must make unpopular decisions for the country's long-term good.

The good news is that we have advantages that our ancestors did not. We have better data and tools to understand the impacts of our policies. We have a more educated population. We benefit from learning from both the successes and mistakes of the past. And we're a heck of a lot richer.

So, what will it take to turn this fiscal ship around? Among other items, it will take bipartisan cooperation to adopt the fiscal rules laid out in the last chapter that would restore fiscal democracy. Obviously, these rules will necessitate spending and tax reform to curb automatic growth, pay our bills more promptly, and enhance transparency to prevent the recurrence of past sins. To demonstrate the shift towards the new regime, it is crucial to show

Beyond Zombie Rule

the public how these reforms can fund new initiatives. These include education and research, providing work subsidies to the long-neglected working class, improving infrastructure, and other projects to bolster the future.

It will take a lot of work, and there will be some takeaways along with the giveaways. But if history has taught us anything, Americans often rise to the occasion better when faced with the biggest challenges, or, as Winston Churchill allegedly said, "Americans will always do the right thing, only after they have tried everything else." Well, we have tried almost everything else, and that's why we are at this fiscal turning point.

Will we learn from our past and begin making decisions that ultimately lead us to a better path? After all, government doesn't exist to reduce its own deficit but, ideally, to enhance the well-being of its citizens. Or will we keep trying to muddle along, living in delusion about the merit of unsustainable policies largely made by past elected officials? Like citizens and leaders in our past fiscal crises recognized, our real crisis is not taking advantage of the opportunities before us.

In summary, today's fiscal turning point may be unavoidable, but it's uncertain that we will handle it well. It has many parallels with two significant historical turning points—the post-Revolutionary period and the Progressive Era—from which we can learn. Those past crises required major fiscal

Beyond Zombie Rule

reforms and unpopular "takeaways" to address the needs of a changing nation. We're at a similar crossroads today, facing issues like mounting debt, outdated tax codes under which our bills are increasingly not being paid, and entitlement programs with unsustainable growth. In addition to restoring fiscal freedom to future voters and lawmakers, critical requirements for addressing these challenges include bipartisan cooperation, fiscal responsibility, and a willingness to make tough choices for long-term benefits.

In the following two chapters, we'll delve deeper into some historical developments that led to our current predicament. First, we'll explore how specific economic theories and expanding expectations of government have contributed to our mounting debt and deficits, helping provide excuses for the irresponsible fiscal policy that led to today's fiscal straitjacket.

Chapter 3: Where Did All This Mess Come From?

I don't worry about the deficit. It is big enough to take care of itself. -- Ronald Reagan

You know how sometimes you look at your bank account and wonder, "How the heck did I end up here?" That's where we are right now with our government. We've got a mountain of debt, deficits as far as the eye can see, a government mainly on autopilot when it comes to spending and a revenue system that falls increasingly short of covering that spending. But how did we get here? As noted by Switzerland's Finance Minister, Karin Keller-Sutter, how did we join those countries that are "so indebted they're hardly able to act anymore?" "[T]ake a look at America," she added, "That's a time bomb." Let's take a trip down memory lane and see if we can't answer those questions.

First things first, we need to look at two key sets of ideas that changed the public's and their representatives' perceptions of what the government could achieve, or more precisely, what restrictions they could lift:

1. Keynesian economics and supply-side theory: These started as legit ways to think about the economy, but politicians twisted them into excuses for spending sprees and tax cuts galore.

2. Unrealistic expectations of what the government should do: Since the 1930s, people have increasingly wanted the government to fix every economic and social problem under the sun. This led to a vast expansion in uncoordinated government programs and the lobbyists and think tank researchers (oops, does that include me?) who get most of their financial support by arguing mainly over what new giveaways the government should provide, but seldom over how to pay for them or do them well.

For decades, Democrats and Republicans have been using these ideas to justify all sorts of permanent government programs and tax cuts while ignoring the increasing imbalance between the two. They've been so busy trying to control the future that they've left coming generations with a big mess to clean up.

Now, let's zoom in on how we got here.

The American Debt Allergy

Let's start with a mind-bending concept: America's relationship with debt. For most of our history, we treated debt like that one weird cousin at family reunions—we acknowledged its existence but tried to avoid it at all costs. Thomas Jefferson and James Madison were so anti-debt they probably wouldn't even play Monopoly. Can you imagine them landing on Boardwalk? "I

Jefferson and Hamilton Playing Monopoly

Beyond Zombie Rule

refuse to go into debt for this property, good sir. I shall pass my turn."

Until 1929, we followed a fairly simple pattern: rack up debt mainly during wars (OK, Jefferson also relented to purchase the Louisiana Territory), then pay it off during good times. It was like a national piggy bank—break it open when needed, then fill it back up when you can.

But then the Great Depression hit, and everything changed.

Enter the Keynesians

John Maynard Keynes showed up and said, "Hey, maybe deficits aren't so bad after all." He argued that governments should spend money during bad times to boost the economy. This was a big deal because it went against everything people thought they knew about balancing budgets. In truth, he wasn't the first, but he provided some excellent economic arguments for how your spending might lead to higher employment opportunities for everyone.

Keynes's idea was simple: the government should spend more to lift the economy when it is down and save when it's up. It's like fiscal yoga—stretch when you're

Keynesian and Supply-Side Economists

tight and contract when you're loose. But politicians usually ignored part two. They were like kids who only heard "eat your dessert" and missed the "after you finish your vegetables" part.

The idea took off in the 1960s when President Kennedy's adviser, Walter Heller, pushed for tax cuts to stimulate the economy. It was like giving the economy a shot of espresso—a quick boost to get things moving.

But here's the problem: once politicians tasted deficit spending, they couldn't stop. Whether the economy was in a recession, exiting one, or entering one, they claimed a constant need for more stimulus. It was like fiscal candy—sweet in the moment but not so great for long-term health.

The Supply-Side Swagger

By the time Ronald Reagan rolled into the White House in 1981, the high inflation and stagnating economy of the 1970s had made Keynesian economics look worse for wear. Reagan and his team decided to let monetary policy handle the inflation problem but needed a new justification for tax cuts, and they found it in supply-side economics.

The basic idea of supply-side economics is that if you cut taxes, people will work harder and invest more, thereby growing the economy. It's like telling people, "If your employer gives you more take-home pay per hour, you'll work more hours, days, or years."

Now, like Keynesian economics, this isn't totally wild. If tax rates are super high (like the 90 percent rate President Reagan remembered paying during World War II), then cutting them might not reduce revenues. But when rates are moderate, cutting rates might even lead people to work or invest less, given their new windfall. Rational supply-side theory agrees with this type of balance when it concludes that distortions are greatest when tax rate increases are cobbled on to existing high tax rates.

The problem is that some folks—looking at you, Wall Street Journal (WSJ) editorial page—took this idea and ran with it. They started arguing for tax cuts all the time, no matter what the rates were or how big the deficit was. It was like fiscal voodoo—keep cutting taxes, and somehow, magically, everything would work out.

Rising Expectations

Unsurprisingly, the public's expectations significantly increased when they learned they didn't have to pay for spending increases or tax cuts. Nor has the public come to expect to pay for emergency spending once crises like 9-11, the Great Recession, and the COVID-19 pandemic hit. These economic theories not only gave some support to this way of thinking, but as we will see in more detail in the next chapter, the idea that giveaway laws could always be easily enacted. The lack of severe economic consequences was also backed up for a long while by things like rising domestic spending paid for by postwar declines in defense spending.

Fast Forward to Today

So here we are in 2024. We've just come through a global pandemic that forced the government to spend trillions of dollars to keep the economy afloat. And, once again, we made no effort to pay for this vast expansion of our national debt, even though the continued retirement of the baby boomers puts steady upward pressure on spending and downward pressure on revenues.

Fiscal Rubik's Cube

The consequences of apparently easy money and costless giveaways extend well beyond deficits. We've got a tax system that's more complicated than a Rubik's Cube and about as fair as a rigged carnival game. Social Security and Medicare run ever larger shortfalls of revenues relative to spending as they struggle to keep up with an aging population. Meanwhile, we've yet to get healthcare expenses, public and private, under control.

Democrats and Republicans effectively conspired to create permanent laws that preempt addressing almost any modern problem.

Furthermore, under a more rational system, we could and should address several serious challenges such as climate change, wage and wealth inequality, technological disruption, global competition, and an aging infrastructure. This chapter illustrates the collaborative efforts of Democrats and Republicans to craft unchangeable laws that together defy fiscal logic. These laws now prohibit people from using the extra money generated by economic growth to solve almost any problem.

There's more. As almost every voter knows, we're trying to solve all these problems with a political system that's more gridlocked than Los Angeles traffic on a Friday afternoon. Congress can barely agree on what day it is, let alone how to tackle these massive challenges.

So, What Now?

Look, we've been in tough spots before. What we need now is some of that old-school American ingenuity to address a problematic but hardly impossible situation. We can restore fiscal democracy by limiting automatic spending growth and maintaining revenues at a current level that, over time, covers any spending level set by law. Those two steps would dramatically simplify enacting various other reforms. Here is an example:

> Welfare reform in the 1990s, whatever you may think of it, was made possible mainly by the gradual erosion, relative to national income, of what in the early 1960s had been the nation's primary welfare program, Aid to Families with Dependent Children (AFDC). Indeed, AFDC even had permanent entitlement status but with limited built-in growth. As a result, by the time of the 1990s reform, it was a mere shadow of itself and had already been largely

replaced with alternatives like the wage subsidy, EITC, that received legislative boosts.

Now, I know what you're thinking: "Easy for you to say, buddy. You're not the one who has to get re-elected." And you're right. Reforming entitlements with considerable built-in growth and raising taxes to pay our bills won't be easy or popular, mainly because they require reneging on excessive promises for spending growth and lower taxes that by now have been baked into current laws. But here's the thing: if we don't make those reforms, we're setting ourselves up for a world of hurt.

Remember how our ancestors faced British taxation without representation? How they weathered the Civil War and two World Wars? How they pulled together during the Great Depression and came out stronger? How they established the Pax Americana, which so far not only prevented a new world war but also defeated Communism and dramatically reduced worldwide poverty. We have the same grit and determination in our DNA.

Recognizing that you and I, not just "others," benefited from the law's excessive promises will be difficult. But the reward is restoring a country that's not just surviving but thriving, and the American Dream is again alive and kicking. Dreaming again and striving for real reform can be much more fun and less dangerous than our current partisan bickering and tribal warfare.

———

> In summary, two factors help explain the origin of America's current fiscal predicament: the

Beyond Zombie Rule

misapplication of Keynesian and supply-side economic theories and the expanding expectations of the government's role once giveaway legislation appeared costless. These ideas provided political justification for a cycle of increasing spending and tax cuts, resulting in mounting debt and deficits. Under current circumstances, entitlement, tax, and political process reforms have become inevitable. However, the quality of their future execution remains uncertain.

Having explored how economic theories became misconstrued in ways that have led to our fiscal challenges, we next take a journey through America's post-war fiscal history, tracing the gradual erosion of fiscal democracy and the increasing constraints on the government's ability to address new challenges. This historical perspective will help us understand why fiscal reform is so difficult politically today, despite the fact that it should be easier economically than it was when we had similar levels of debt relative to our current income but a significantly poorer nation at the end of World War II.

Chapter 4: The Gradual Demise of Fiscal Democracy: A Post-War Fiscal Odyssey

*"Prisoner, tell me, who was it that wrought this unbreakable chain?" "It was I," said the Prisoner, "who carefully forged this chain. I thought my invincible power would hold the world captive leaving me in a freedom undisturbed. Thus night and day I worked at the chain with huge fires and cruel hard strokes. When at last the work was done and the links were complete and unbreakable, I found that it held me in its grip." --- Rabindranath Tagore, **Gitanjali***

Our two political parties have been busy forging legal chains around spending and tax policy for some time, preventing the government from addressing new needs and opportunities. These efforts can be summarized across four eras.

The Era of Easy Finance: 1945-1981: When Money Grew on Trees

Picture this: It's the early period after World War II, and America is riding high. The economy is booming, people are optimistic and politicians are generous. We're ready to splurge.

For the next 26 years, the government started handing out goodies left and right. Social Security increases? Check. Medicare? You got

Beyond Zombie Rule

it. Medicaid? Of course. More Great Society programs? Why not! The programs led to the establishment of numerous new executive branch departments. It was like Christmas morning, and Uncle Sam was playing Santa Claus.

They weren't just spending money on domestic programs. They also started cutting taxes like there was no tomorrow. Almost all tax bills over the past eight decades have been net tax cuts, even Lyndon Johnson's temporary surtax to help pay for the Vietnam war. Democrats and Republicans competed to determine who could propose the most innovative tax measures. It resembled a political version of "The Price is Right," in which everyone emerged victorious, and "Any Price is Right!"

Political Game Show

You might wonder, "How did they afford all this?" The extreme versions of the economic theories discussed provided only political justification but didn't make the numbers add up. It was a fortunate period for a politician—never looking like you had to pay for anything, as large surpluses would have developed if Congress hadn't legislated new spending and tax cuts.

Beyond Zombie Rule

1. Taxes had been raised significantly during World War II, and as defense spending was reduced in cycles after that war and the Korean and Vietnam conflicts, a considerable amount was transferred to domestic policy without raising taxes.

2. The economy was growing faster than a teenager in a growth spurt.

3. Inflation and real economic growth sneakily pushed people into higher tax brackets (hello, bracket creep!), raising taxes to fund new tax cuts.

4. For the first few generations receiving Social Security and Medicare, Congress legislated large windfalls of lifetime benefits above lifetime taxes (more on this later).

But here's the thing: while everyone was partying like it was the early 1920s, they were also setting up future generations, who had no vote in the matter, for a massive hangover. Unlike almost all legislation in the nation's previous history, including most New Deal legislation, new enactments in this period often provided for eternal automatic growth. Think of when your entertainment came from simply buying a TV, and then you added cable TV providers, whose yearly

A Skunk at a Garden Party

charges rose without you understanding why.

And raising taxes to pay for it all? It was as popular with politicians as a skunk at a garden party.

The Era of Fiscal Straitjackets: 1982-1997: The Party's Over, Folks

Remember how I said there'd be a hangover? In 1974, the nation's debt relative to its national income hit a nadir, and new things started looking less free. President Carter was unpopular with many old-gang Democrats, especially when the engineer in him wanted cost-benefit analysis to justify government programs.

By the late 1970s, high inflation and low growth (stagflation) had hit like a wrecking ball, and Reagan swooped in with his big tax cuts in 1981. It was the last hurrah of that giveaway era, but boy, did it make things worse budgetarily. Suddenly, everyone was staring at continual deficits relative to our national income that were bigger than anything seen in peacetime.

This is when things almost got real. Politicians started talking about "deficit reduction" as the hottest new trend. Reagan, Bush Sr., and Clinton sat down with Congress after 1981 and hashed some pretty nasty but bipartisan deals. They increased taxes and cut spending, often eliciting strong negative reactions by advocacy groups. The deals weren't that big one-by-one, but they combined with limited amounts of new legislative giveaways to slow down the growth of the national debt.

Beyond Zombie Rule

They also showed just how tricky it was becoming to manage the country's finances. It was like trying to turn a cruise ship using only sails—possible but painfully slow and inadequate for the long voyage. Still, deficit reduction legislation in 1982, 1983 (Social Security), 1984, 1990, 1993, and possibly 1997 brought a brief ray of sunshine and even some budget surpluses at the end of the century.

But don't get too excited about this calm before the storm. They still failed to address the long-term imbalances built into the future, especially with baby boomers soon moving from maximum earning to retirement years and healthcare costs still rising relatively unconstrained.

The Era of Two Santas: 1998-2010: Double the Santas, Double the Fun?

In the late 1970s, Jude Wanniski, one of the WSJ editors, argued that to win elections, Republicans needed to play Santa with tax cuts the way he asserted Democrats got to play Santa with spending increases. His "Two Santa Theory" helps summarize how both parties could mutually overpromise and box in progress for the nation.

Two Political Santas

By 1995, Republicans had captured the House

Beyond Zombie Rule

of Representatives for only the third time since 1932. Now, they could test Wanniski's theory and a pledge never to raise taxes anywhere for any reason.

It wasn't just one Santa—oh no, now we have two! It was as if we were witnessing two grownups competing for attention while attempting to distribute gifts.

Given the temporary surpluses of the late 1990s, George W. Bush calculated that with "compassionate conservatism," he could be both Santas. He signed bills that cut taxes, increased defense spending, bumped up domestic spending, and added prescription drug coverage to Medicare. Measured relative to our national income, he probably qualifies for the Guinness Book of Records as "the U.S. president who gave away the most money without paying for it." Surpluses quickly turned into sizable deficits.

Meanwhile, the retirement crisis kept looming like a big, gray storm cloud as the baby boomers were to first become eligible for Social Security in 2008. Bush tried to spend "political capital" to fix Social Security. Still, a poorly designed proposal and Democrats' unwillingness to give an inch on rising Social Security benefits doomed this effort to failure. Pfft, that's still a problem for the future.

Obama's election followed the Great Recession, which began in 2007. Suddenly, the government had to step in and save the day, leading to deficits so large they made previous ones look like pocket change. Not surprisingly, there was no willingness to pay for those enormous increases in national debt in the future.

Beyond Zombie Rule

With the Affordable Care Act (ACA), Obama reduced health insurance gaps in the population but failed to rein in existing health cost growth. By later removing some ACA tax increases, Republicans added to deficits. When it came to addressing those underlying budget issues, the political gridlock was so bad you could see it from space. Leaders in both parties often followed the rule to vote unanimously by party on any important legislation. Their mantra was, "If proposed by the other party, it must be bad, and, even if good, we can't pass anything that would give the other party too much credit."

The Prisoner's Dilemma Era: 2011-Present

The classic dilemma, known as the Prisoner's Dilemma, had by now completely trapped politicians. In shorthand, "If you lead, you lose, and if you don't lead, society loses." Suppose you're a Republican who favors any tax increase or a Democrat who favors any cut in entitlement spending. In that case, someone in your party will come after you in the primaries, and even if you survive, the party leaders probably won't give you a favorable committee assignment in Congress.

As we stumbled out of the Great Recession, nursing our economic hangover, a new force emerged on the political scene: the Tea Party. For a brief period, these folks were "mad as hell" about government deficits and "wouldn't take it anymore."

The Tea Party had some valid points about fiscal responsibility, but once in office, they also had about as much flexibility as a steel rod. It became OK under the Republican "no new taxes, ever" pledge to add to deficits, and their willingness to shut down the government made finding solutions improbable. They soon turned their anger to cultural warfare issues—you know, if you can't win on money issues, how about regulating personal behavior?

Politicians faced a classic dilemma. In shorthand, "If you lead, you lose, and if you don't lead, society loses."

Obama's presidency, especially after 2011 when he no longer had a Democratic majority in both Houses of Congress, saw one budget battle after another. One result? Congress ramped up efforts, first began in 1990, to "sequester" or "cut" an equal arbitrary amount from mainly discretionary programs. This is about as precise as using a sledgehammer to hang pictures. Investments in things like education and infrastructure took a beating. Despite fiscal democracy's ongoing decline, most mandatory spending remained exempt and steadily increased as a percentage of the budget.

Despite these measures and a post-ACA stalemate in enacting any new significant tax cuts or spending increases, the national debt grew relative to national income, with such growth only adding to the growth incurred during the Great Recession..

Beyond Zombie Rule

There was one critical difference between Republicans and Democrats. Democrats kept trying to sustain the growth in existing entitlements without paying for it. Still, on some occasions they maintained some allegiance to the pay-as-you-go (PAYGO) rules first implemented in 1990 for new mandatory spending or tax legislation. Republicans didn't accept PAYGO for tax cuts and kept their stance on never raising taxes.

> **Then along came Trump in 2016, adding a new chapter to "deficits don't matter."**

Then along came Trump in 2016, adding a new chapter to "deficits don't matter." He offered yet another tax cut and, to boost, a promise never to touch Social Security and Medicare. The Tax Cuts and Jobs Act of 2017 aimed to stimulate the economy and bring U.S. multinational corporations' tax rates down to match those of many other developed nations. Critics said it was another giveaway to the rich that would worsen our fiscal problems. Theoretically, future Congresses would feel compelled to pay for some of it. You've got it—yet another set of cans kicked down the road.

And just when we thought things couldn't get crazier, 2020 brought the COVID-19 pandemic. Sure, it was necessary to keep the economy from completely tanking, but it also sent our national debt soaring to levels not seen since we were fighting the Nazis.

Beyond Zombie Rule

Suddenly, we were once again spending trillions of dollars at the speed of an "economic crisis." Biden tried to expand spending on a more permanent basis. Still, compromise in the misnamed Inflation Reduction Act of 2022 led mainly to an effort to finance the development of alternative energy sources with some PAY-GO.

However, there was no PAY-GO for the extraordinary COVID-19-related spending for the years 2020 through 2022, significant presidential deficit-increasing decisions in regulating and administering programs like student debt, and, of course, the continued rise in automatic spending from mandatory programs, building on yet higher bases.

The Path Forward: Will We Finally Face the Music?

So, here we are, staring down the barrel of serious fiscal challenges. We've got an aging population, off-the-chart healthcare costs, a large national debt with a gravitational pull, rising interest costs, and a political system as functional as a chocolate teapot.

What's the solution? You've heard some in previous chapters, but I'll organize it here in terms of honesty, process, and, yes, new investment.

1. **Honesty.** We—citizens, not just politicians—need to face the facts. This mess requires entitlement reform, tax increases, and spending cuts—the fiscal policy equivalent of eating your vegetables, going to the gym, and flossing all at once.

Beyond Zombie Rule

2. **Process.** Our current political system is about as good at solving long-term problems as a goldfish at calculus. We need a new budget process that focuses on the long run and disallows any unsustainable spending or tax giveaways, whether new or old, that require future Congresses to come up with the takeaways.

3. **New Investment.** Reform must reorient budget decision-making toward finding the best ways to tax and spend. Deficit reduction is not enough. Strengthening our country in the long run requires attention to areas such as education, infrastructure, support for workers, and scientific research—the critical stuff that our two political parties have been squeezing out for decades.

We've faced enormous challenges before. Remember World War II? The Civil Rights Movement? Making it through the Great Depression without resorting to tyranny? A rising economy makes all sorts of new things possible. As I keep pointing out, this is mainly a political issue, not an economic one.

Elected Republicans and Democrats have spent decades forging this "chain" of fiscal commitments. But it's less necessary to break the links than to remove the locks and recognize that the chains are uncomfortable and don't protect us. This crisis provides an opportunity to think long-term about building an incredible and sustainable future, not just from election to election.

_____

Beyond Zombie Rule

In summary, we can divide U.S. fiscal policy since World War II into four distinct eras. Following an era of easy financing and numerous domestic programs, we entered a period of fiscal constraints. Despite efforts to reduce the near-term deficit, the long-run debt problem, derived from future commitments built into the law, remained unaddressed. By the turn of the new century, debt and deficits started soaring due to a combination of abandonment of the types of constraints enacted from 1982 to 1997, ever larger automatic entitlement growth, two significant tax cuts, yet more healthcare expansions that weren't paid for, and enormous outlays and tax cuts for the Great Recession and the COVID-19 crisis. Both major political parties continue to significantly contribute to the current fiscal predicament, and without greater efforts at honesty, process reform, and a renewed focus on investment in the nation's future, finding a solution seems unlikely.

In effect, the gradual erosion of fiscal democracy has been a long process, with roots stretching back decades. In the next chapter, we'll explore how those developments led to a shift in policy from controlling the present to managing the future and how that has fundamentally altered how our government operates. We'll explore the unintended consequences of this change and why it's become so

Beyond Zombie Rule

difficult for policymakers to address new challenges and opportunities.

Chapter 5: From Controlling the Present to Controlling the Future

"We're forgetting how to fly." -- Rory Kay, a pilot and an FAA committee co-chair

Imagine you're on a plane, and the autopilot's been engaged to keep the nose up since takeoff. Everything seems OK, but the pilots  have been relying on autopilot for so long that they're starting to forget how to fly the plane, which continues to rise well past its assigned flight level of 18,000 feet. Scary, right? Well, buckle up because we've got a similar problem with our government's budget. Congress has put it on autopilot and has forgotten how to manage either direction or level. Yikes!

Let's recap a bit and then explain in detail how efforts to control the future have created this huge mess. There's always been an issue with politicians potentially being profligate year after year and throwing money around like confetti (though there's plenty of that). However, in the last few decades, there has been a profound shift in the way Congress approaches government spending and taxes. And it's made federal budget policymaking completely unworkable.

Mandating Ever More

Back in the day, most government spending was "discretionary." That's fancy budget-speak for "each year we decide again how much to spend." The president and Congress would hash it out, deciding which existing programs to fund or kick to the curb and which new ones to create. They'd pass these things called appropriations bills—twelve of them today, to be exact—covering everything from defense to education to food safety.

But then, as we've seen, along came this other type of spending: "mandatory." Social Security, Medicare, Food Stamps (now called SNAP), disability insurance, and many other programs now fall into this category. Because Congress makes most mandatory programs and tax subsidies permanent, they fundamentally change expectations among households and businesses. Think of them like those digital subscriptions you forget to cancel—they keep charging you—until you finally remember to log in and hit "unsubscribe." But wait, you can't even do that by yourself, as three adults in your household (the Senate, the House, and the President) each have veto power.

Here's an even bigger game changer: the largest programs were designed not simply to be permanent but to grow automatically. Also, forever. Each year, they would provide more generous benefits to more eligible people, often increasing faster than people's incomes or the economy. Imagine if your family's gym

Beyond Zombie Rule

membership fee, which dates back to your grandparents, were to increase annually at a faster rate than your family's income.

The result? Mandatory spending and interest on the debt have been eating up larger and larger shares of the federal budget pie: in the 1960s, 36% of outlays or less; in 2023, 72%. The Congressional Budget Office projects a further decline in the discretionary spending share from its 2023 level of 28 percent. Remember the graph on fiscal democracy in Chapter 1? Mandatory spending and interest alone absorb all revenues, and soon, even

Fiscal Pac-Man

more. We can run deficits without even appropriating anything! Entitlements have become the Pac-Man of the federal budget, gobbling up everything in sight.

Now, you might be thinking, "Why don't they just cut these programs?" Here's the thing: in budget land, a "cut" doesn't always mean what you think it means. In legislative budget-speak, we now measure a cut in relation to what the law promises, not in relation to last year's appropriations. (When spending was almost entirely appropriations, the two measures were the same.) If Congress reduces benefits merely to make some growth rate sustainable, that's declared a "cut" by pundits, reporters, and, particularly, advocates and interest groups. The last make their living partly out of stoking controversy and telling us how much we need them to protect our entitlements. It's as if a previous boss assured you of significant annual raises, but a new boss determined that the company could only provide smaller raises. Technically, you're still getting more money, but it feels like a loss.

In addition to all of this, there are "tax expenditures"—tax subsidies, which are essentially disguised government spending. They come in many forms: deductions, credits, and other write-offs that lower the tax that households and businesses pay.

Mandatory spending and interest ate up 36% or less of outlays in the 1960s; in 2023, 72%.

Some of these tax breaks are hugely popular, like the tax-free treatment of employer-provided health care and the capital gains exclusion. They're as important to many Americans as Social Security or Medicare. And guess what? Just like those entitlement programs, most are permanent and grow in cost year after year.

So, we've got all these programs that keep growing, usually regardless of any effort to measure whether we need or can afford them. Think of the 2024 presidential campaign. Both Donald Trump and Kamala Harris promised to protect our Social Security and Medicare benefits. But what the heck does that mean? Of course, we shouldn't cut benefits on which current retirees rely.

Beyond Zombie Rule

But protect unsustainable growth rates? And why is that the "right" growth rate if the money could be used better elsewhere? It's like a garden where the weeds have taken over, and nobody remembers how to use the weed-whacker.

Both Donald Trump and Kamala Harris promised to protect our Social Security and Medicare benefits. But what the heck does that mean?

But wait, there's more! (Isn't there always?) We're now facing a demographic time bomb. Remember how the "baby boom" population born between 1946 and 1964 was followed by a baby bust population. Well, the boomers are retiring now. And that's a double whammy for the budget—more people claim Social Security and Medicare benefits, while fewer workers per retiree pay the taxes required to fund them.

It would be eye-watering if we had to pay for all of these programs with a single transparent tax, such as the Social Security payroll tax. In the late 1960s, when mandatory programs were about 5% of GDP, you could fund them with about a 10% tax rate on the Social Security earnings base. Today, at about 15% of GDP, you'd need a 30% tax rate. Add future mandatory spending growth, rising interest costs, discretionary spending, and payments for the next crises, and you can see where we are headed. Ouch!

Beyond Zombie Rule

To put it another way, think about how much money in today's dollars a typical couple with average income and life expectancy would need at age 65 in a retirement account earning interest to cover what they'll get from Social Security and Medicare alone. In 1960, it would have been about $350,000; in 2010, $1.1 million; in 2030, $1.5 million. By 2050, retiring millennial couples are scheduled to get $2.1 million. And that doesn't even include potential nursing home costs covered by Medicaid and other government benefits.!

So, what's causing all this growth? For retirement programs, it's a perfect storm:

1. Benefits automatically increase as wages go up.
2. People live longer, so they collect benefits for more years.
3. As birth rates fall, there are fewer workers to support each retiree.

The first two items alone—wage "indexing" and more years of benefits—require Social Security to continue growing faster than GDP after it has already been doing so for close to a century.

Healthcare faces the same pressures from longer lives and fewer workers. Plus, our health insurance system often lets patients and doctors decide what treatment to provide without regard for what other taxpayers need to fork out to cover the cost. It's like splitting a group bill at an expensive restaurant, where Joe has ten drinks, and Matilda insists on the Kobe beef. Essentially, no major federal health insurance program, such as Medicare, Medicaid,

Beyond Zombie Rule

exchange subsidies under Obamacare, or the tax break for employer-provided insurance, have been budgeted to control costs.

And it's not just the federal government facing this problem. State governments are in the same boat. They're spending more and more on Medicaid, which, for many years, has absorbed half of all growth in state spending while eating into education and other budgets. They've also struggled to pay hefty employee pension and health benefits.

A Whole New Ballgame

Now, here's where things get fascinating (or terrifying, depending on your perspective). Throughout most of U.S. history, this wasn't such a big deal. Why? When spending was mostly discretionary, revenues grew almost yearly as the economy expanded. So, even if starting out in a deficit situation, over the long run the budget was scheduled to generate surpluses. To move out of a deficit situation, policymakers just needed temporarily to avoid legislating an increase in outlays or a tax cut. No legislation identified as spending "cuts" or tax "increases" was required.

This meant politicians could set new budgetary directions based on the needs of the time (or the whims of voters) without having to "cut" a program and appear to renege on some existing promise. Most of the time, they had to increase spending or cut taxes to avoid problems from growing surpluses.

Beyond Zombie Rule

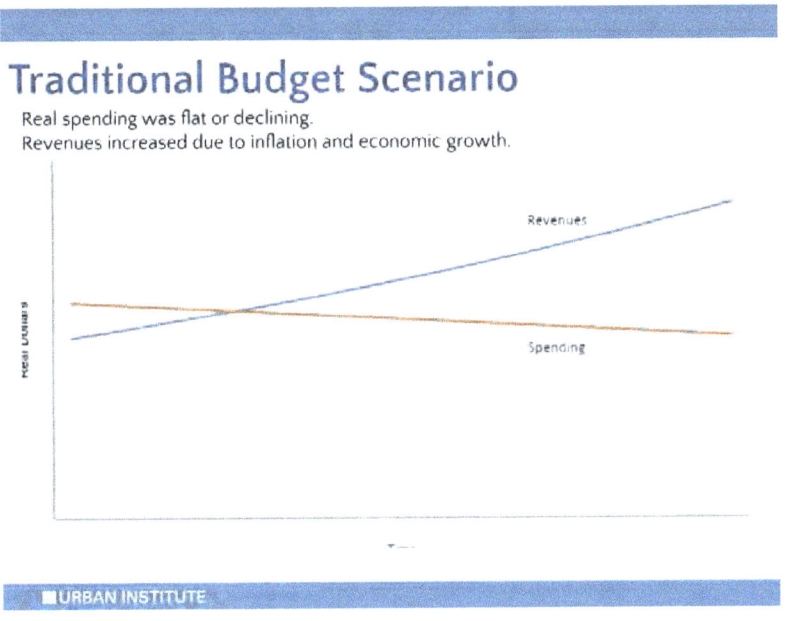

But now? We're in a whole new ballgame. As this automatic growth has compounded, the law now schedules mandatory spending plus interest alone to exceed aggregate revenues for the first time in our history. Permanently. Therefore, future expected revenue growth cannot offset existing build-in growth in spending, much less any new spending increase or tax cut. Remember, we're measuring cuts relative to what the current law requires, not relative to what government provided previously.

Beyond Zombie Rule

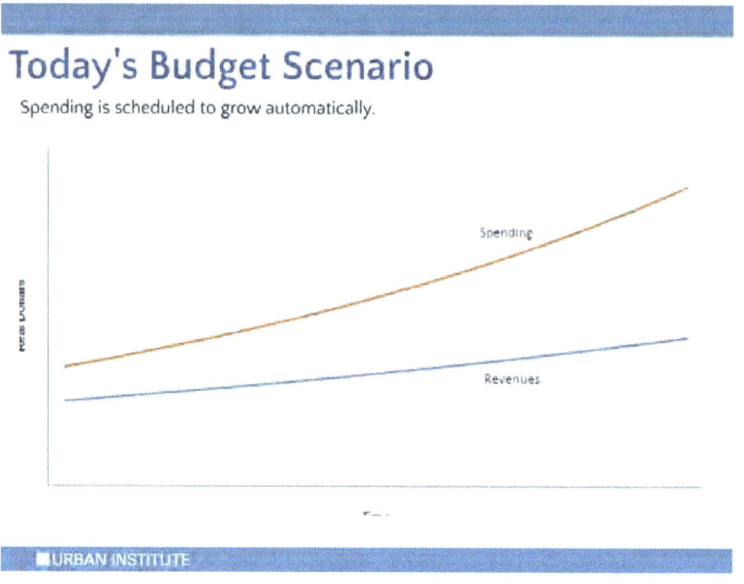

Believe it or not, this fundamental shift, as diagrammed in the two figures above, is driving much of the fiscal angst, confusion, and disappointment that confront elected officials in almost all developed nations.

This budgetary chaos, in turn, has led to political chaos. In the past, policymakers could create a sustainable budget simply by not legislating much higher discretionary spending or lower taxes for a brief period. In fact, under current law, there were only long-term budget surpluses in the way that CBO now measures it. After all, revenues grew at roughly the same rate as the economy, but spending did not. Thus, no matter what the starting point, future revenues would eventually surpass some fixed level of spending. But that strategy doesn't work anymore.

Beyond Zombie Rule

Some argue that higher economic growth can solve this problem by boosting revenue growth. Liberals use this argument to suggest they might not need to reform programs like Social Security after all, while conservatives use it to argue that tax cuts always pay for themselves by creating additional economic growth.

But here's the reality check: economic growth provides limited gains in today's environment. Yes, it boosts revenues relative to scheduled discretionary spending. However, the design of the largest and most important growth programs ensures that they expand at a faster pace as the economy grows. So, economic growth means that spending automatically increases along with revenues, which then does little to solve our problem.

The law now schedules mandatory spending plus interest alone to exceed aggregate revenues for the first time in our history.

It's like being on a treadmill that keeps speeding up as you run faster—no matter how fast you run, you're not getting anywhere.

Facing Reality

So, what does all this mean? We're facing economic and political consequences that we can't solve by focusing on deficits alone. We need to rethink how we approach government spending and taxes.

Beyond Zombie Rule

We need to ask ourselves some tough questions:

- Do we need so many programs to grow automatically forever?

- Can we design a sustainable social safety net that does an even better job of protecting people who fall behind?

- How do we balance the needs of future retirees with the need to invest in workers and the young?

- Can we create a tax system that's both fair and sufficient to fund the government we want?

While these are challenging questions, I think we know the answers. And so do most of our elected officials. Jean-Claude Juncker, a Prime Minister for Luxembourg, once admitted, "We all know what to do; we just don't know how to get re-elected after we've done it." Of course, the details matter, such as ensuring that reform doesn't mean replacing one predetermined future with another. But if we don't start grappling with the tradeoffs soon, based on such principles as orienting resources to the greatest needs and best payoffs, we will quickly find ourselves in a fiscal hole so deep we can't climb out. And it doesn't take a financial collapse: programs designed increasingly for yesteryear cause enormous inequity and waste.

Remember those pilots who forget how to fly because they rely too much on autopilot? Well, we need to turn off the fiscal autopilot and start actively managing our national finances again. The transition might be uncomfortable politically, but once completed,

Beyond Zombie Rule

it makes it easier for Congress to engage in giveaways. In fact, it would be unavoidable given the size of surpluses that would otherwise arise.

Next time you hear politicians promising more giveaways without explaining how they'll pay for them, remember there's no such thing as a free lunch. Or a free Social Security check. Or a free Medicare benefit. Everything has a cost, and somebody has to pay those bills sooner or later.

It's time to face reality. Otherwise, we might find ourselves on a fiscal flight path that ends in a crash landing. And trust me, that's one in-flight movie no one wants to see.

In summary, mandatory spending programs that grow automatically have replaced the U.S. government's system of mostly discretionary spending. Future spending will indefinitely outpace revenue growth due to this profound change, demographic shifts, and rising healthcare costs. This new paradigm explains today's extraordinary political inflexibility and inability to address new challenges.

Having explored how our government has shifted from controlling the present to trying to control the future, let's turn to some deadly consequences, starting with economic ones in the next chapter.

Chapter 6: The Four Deadly Economic Consequences

"Some people create their own storms and then get upset when it rains." — Anonymous

Hey there, fiscal policy fans! Remember when Herbert Hoover said, "Prosperity is just around the corner"? Well, we're still looking for that corner, and our fiscal GPS seems to be on the fritz. Let's dive deeper into the four deadly economic consequences of our current fiscal mess, shall we?

First, our fiscal problem isn't like some disease suddenly attacking us. It's more like we're a species that's been binge-eating junk food for a long time and still reaching for the cookie jar. We've been gorging on deficit spending, and now we're facing some severe indigestion.

Fiscal GPS on the Fritz

So, how did we get here? In previous chapters, we've shown how it started with some well-intentioned ideas: expand social welfare (because helping people is good, right?), use Keynesian economics to keep the economy humming during recessions (sounds smart!), and cut taxes to encourage work and saving (who doesn't like paying less tax?). But we've taken these ideas to the extreme.

Beyond Zombie Rule

Then we saw how Congress set our spending to grow faster than our revenue forever—or at least until the economy collapses. Let's now break down the four deadly economic consequences of this fiscal fiasco:

1. Rising and Unsustainable Levels of Debt

Remember when your parents told you money doesn't grow on trees? Someone forgot to tell the government. Our national debt is skyrocketing to all-time highs as a share of our national income. It's like we've maxed out the national credit card, applied for a few more, maxed those out, too, and now we're eyeing the neighbor's wallet.

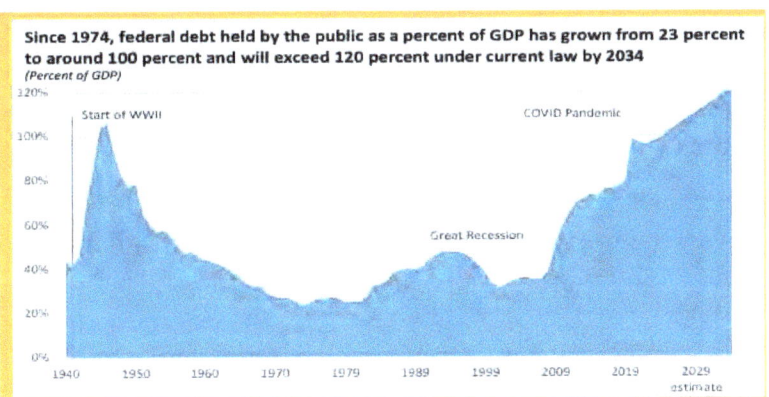

The Congressional Budget Office (CBO) keeps projecting doom-and-gloom scenarios where our debt-to-GDP ratio goes through the roof. Of course, this won't happen because, at some point, our lenders (hello, China!) will stop enabling our debt addiction.

Beyond Zombie Rule

The scary part? We don't know exactly when this day of reckoning will come. It could be next year, or it could be in a decade. But when it happens, it won't be a pretty sight. We're toying with potential economic crises, such as plummeting dollar value and inflation, that make your grocery bill look like a phone number.

Consider that by 2034, nearly one-quarter of your taxes will go for nothing more than interest payments on the debt.

But even if there's no sudden collapse—the dollar does remain the world's currency—consider that by 2034, nearly one-quarter of your taxes will go for nothing more than interest payments on debt. Is this what conservatives, liberals, and moderates all want from their government—spending more on interest than children, defense, or any other crucial government function?

Wait, you've heard this prediction about skyrocketing interest costs before. So, what's different today? While our national debt quadrupled as a share of GDP from 1980 until the early 2020s, the interest rate fell by about three-quarters over the same period. Hence, federal net interest payments didn't rise relative to GDP. Those days are gone. After hitting an extraordinarily low point during COVID-19, the interest rate has started to rise, not fall.

Beyond Zombie Rule

Now, rising debt AND the higher interest rates on all that old debt add to the government's interest costs.

But wait, there's more! This mountain of debt and its associated interest costs are more than just a problem for the government. It affects all of us because it squeezes out other revenue sources and threatens higher interest rates on businesses and home purchases when no one wants to buy all this debt. We're playing with fire.

2. Less Ability to Combat Recession and Address New Emergencies

Remember when the government swept like a fiscal superhero during the Great Recession and the COVID-19 pandemic? Yes, we spent trillions to avoid worse economic downturns, but we never paid for it—before or afterward. When debt equals our income, our ability to respond weakens significantly compared to when it's a small fraction.

It's like we've used up all our sick days at work, and now that autumn has started, we know we're likely to catch one flu bug or another. We can't afford to take time off, but we also can't afford not to.

And it's not just recessions that need to be addressed. What about natural disasters? Another pandemic? A significant cybersecurity threat? Another defense peril? Our rising debt, combined with our precommitment of all future revenues, leaves us dangerously limited in responding to future crises.

Beyond Zombie Rule

Consider our government's situation this way: Suppose you keep borrowing to pay for significant repairs to your house, never pay in advance for insurance, and are now in debt up to your eyeballs. What are you going to do when a big storm does severe damage to your already leaky roof?

3. A Budget for a Declining Nation

Even if we somehow avoid an economic meltdown and manage the new crises that always arise over time—the two items above—we're still in hot water. Our current budget is a recipe for national decline. While we spend a lot, we spend less and less on things that help us grow and prosper.

Here are three examples:

1. **Crumbs for Children**: The federal government spends peanuts on kids compared to older folks, even though kids, on average, are more likely to be poor than their retired grandparents. "Sorry, kiddos, maybe we'll make it up to you when you're old," we tell the next generation. Good luck until then!"

   This is shortsighted. These kids are our future workforce, innovators, and leaders. Shortchanging their education and development is like eating our seed corn and wondering why nothing's growing.

2. **Investing Less**: Remember when America used to do new, big, impressive things like going to the moon? Now we can barely afford to fix our potholes. Our children's math and

language skills lag significantly behind those of other nations; our roads and bridges are in disrepair; our power grid is at risk; and our public transportation system pales in comparison to that of many other developed nations. It's like we're trying to compete in a Formula 1 race with a 1950s car.

3. **Socioeconomic Mobility? What's That?:** The American Dream is looking like the American Pipe Dream. Our budget mainly subsidizes consumption, not programs that help people move up the economic ladder. We're giving the cold shoulder to those who have fallen behind, including the working class and the young.

Consider the billions we spend on tax breaks for homeownership and retirement. A first-time homebuyer credit would do much more to expand homeownership than an interest deduction for wealthy owners of second homes. Our retirement plan subsidies do little for those with median or lower wages—that is, for those who can most use them.

This lack of mobility isn't just unfair; it's terrible for the economy. When people can't move up, talent gets wasted, innovation suffers, and the economy grows more slowly. We're leaving money on the table—lots of it.

Beyond Zombie Rule

4. Broken Government with Antiquated Systems

Our government isn't just broken; it's running on Windows 95 while the rest of the world uses quantum computers. We designed our tax and social welfare systems for a country that no longer exists.

Windows 95 vs. Quantum Computing

Take Social Security, for example. Congress enacted Social Security at a time when people generally lived shorter lives and retired later in life. In 1940, the average worker retired at age 68 and had a much shorter life expectancy. If people retired today with the same remaining life expectancy as the 1940 retiree, they would retire at about age 77 on average. Now, I'm not suggesting that 77 should be the retirement age, but something's got to give.

People with average life expectancies are now eligible for old age benefits for about one-third of their adult lives, even as the decline in the birth rate has reduced the number of workers who support each retiree. A couple with an average life expectancy can expect benefits for nearly three decades. You've heard a similar story when it is projected that one or another of a couple is likely to live past age 90.

No one can get these numbers to work—more precisely, for the promised benefits to add up to anywhere near the revenues

Beyond Zombie Rule

available—as reflected in the near-term exhaustion of the Social Security and Medicare trust funds. Despite this, Congress continues to prioritize increasing retirement benefits over any other function. It's like we designed a 100-yard dash, ended up in a marathon, and closed the track to all other events.

A couple with an average life expectancy can expect benefits for nearly three decades.

What about the way we calculate benefits? It's based on a family structure that wasn't even an accurate stereotype for many when benefits were first paid in 1940—a working husband and a stay-at-home wife with children. Today, that 1940s-established structure of additional benefits for spouses without any additional contribution creates marriage bonuses. But then it penalizes many similarly-earning spouses and single individuals who contribute to survivor and spousal benefits but do not receive them. When married couples are younger and often do have kids living with them, the welfare structure (wage subsidies, food stamps, Medicaid) does just the opposite and provides huge marriage penalties. Even after decades, we have yet to reform this absurd set of family policies.

Or look at our healthcare system. We spend way more on treating chronic conditions than on preventing them. It's like we're more interested in mopping up the basement than in preventing its continual flooding.

Don't even get me started on our tax system. It's got more loopholes than a crochet convention. Our tax code (and related commentary), now over 70,000 pages long, is full of special provisions, added over the years, that unfairly benefit special interests. The result is a system that is

Einstein Deciphering Taxes

inefficient, unfair, and susceptible to manipulation by those who can afford clever accountants and lawyers.

Here's what should be the deal-breaker: We're spending ever more billions to keep clunky old systems running—money that could be better spent on, oh, I don't know, actually helping people. How about orienting resources according to needs, such as those of a working class that has lost its faith in government?

At a Crossroads

We're in a fiscal mess of epic proportions, and it's getting worse by the day. Our debt is skyrocketing and our ability to handle economic crises is waning. Even if we manage the debt sustainably, our pre-commitment of all future revenues hinders our ability to adapt to future events.

Still, the bad news, in a way, is good news. Each of these four major economic problems is self-imposed. We did this to ourselves, so we are empowered to fix it. The real question is, do we have the political will?

The future provides challenges and opportunities. We can make the environment dirtier or cleaner. We can ignore or help those left behind as the technological revolution, including AI and automation, reshapes our economy. We can create powerful friends or enemies as rising global prosperity increases worldwide trade and income.

The bad news, in a way, is good news. Our major economic problems are self-imposed.

With fiscal policies stuck in the past, we cannot adapt well to these outside forces or the deadly economic consequences of policies created by the government itself. We continue to argue about tax provisions and entitlement programs as if it's 1980, despite the world's rapid changes. We're at a crossroads, folks. We can no longer hope things will sort themselves out but must start building a fiscal foundation to support a strong, prosperous America for generations to come.

Beyond Zombie Rule

After all, we don't want future generations to look back at us and wonder, "What were they thinking?" We want them to say, "They saw the problems, they faced them head-on, and they fixed them."

> *In summary, America's fiscal mess creates four deadly economic consequences: unsustainable debt levels, reduced ability to respond to economic crises, a budget that promotes national decline, and outdated government systems. These issues stem from decades of unchecked spending, tax cuts, and failure to adapt policies to changing demographics and economic realities. A political will to reform can fix the dire situation.*
>
> *Having explored the economic consequences of our fiscal policies, we next turn to three deadly political headaches that make it challenging for our leaders to address these issues effectively. Understanding these political hurdles is crucial if we hope to overcome them and chart a path toward fiscal responsibility, sustainability, and a chance at upper mobility for all citizens.*

Chapter 7: Three Deadly Political Headaches

We can't fix it because it's broken, and we can't break it because then we'd have to fix it. — Anonymous

You know how sometimes you inherit a mess from your predecessors and think, "Gee, thanks a lot, guys"? That's what's happening with our government now. We've got three severe political headaches or deadly dilemmas, making it very hard for our leaders to fix our money problems and be honest with us. These headaches are also making politics more divisive than a barroom brawl.

Though my focus is on the U.S., most of the developed world suffers from the same three political disorders:

1. The "Fiscal Freedom" Nosedive

2. The "Political Prisoner's Dilemma"

3. The "Can't Fix What's Already Broken" Blues

You've already heard a bit about each of these, so I'll be brief. However, it's important to understand the connections between all three and the need for a collective solution.

Beyond Zombie Rule

Headache #1: The "Fiscal Freedom" Nosedive

Imagine you're a kid, and your parents can't give you an allowance to spend how you see fit because they have signed contracts to pay out more than all the wages they ever expect to receive. They also don't want to work more than they do now. That's basically what's happening with our government's budget. As previously discussed, existing programs already have commitments to receive all incoming funds, including additional amounts arising from economic growth. That leaves minimal space for new initiatives or challenges. Could you imagine our founders attempting to allocate all future revenues, and even more, indefinitely? Our modern legislators have added those obligations to the law, but not the Constitution.

James Madison would be appalled at how the checks and balances he so admired have been turned upside down. Instead of requiring a type of supermajority—generally, support by the House, Senate, and President—to expand government—now it takes a supermajority to stop it from expanding automatically.

James Madison's Lament

Look back at the first figure in this book on fiscal democracy's decline. Back in the day, politicians had more wiggle room to create new programs or cut taxes. Now? Not so much. Congress already commits approximately 100 percent of revenues before its members enter the Capitol at the start of a new session. If they merely maintain discretionary spending at its current real level and let mandatory spending to grow automatically as a share of national income and total outlays, they will commit 108 percent of revenues in approximately ten years. Once again, of course, this projection means that no unpaid-for crisis hits in the meantime.

Instead of requiring a type of supermajority to expand government, now it takes a supermajority to stop it from expanding automatically.

As a result of these commitments, both liberals and conservatives spend little time examining the broader goals of government or how to make it work better. They spend much time defending and repeating past legislative achievements. If one type of tax cut or social spending seemed to work in the past, they seem to think that even more of the same, whether built-in or through new legislation, is always better.

Even though total spending is now far greater than receipts, proposals for more giveaways keep appearing. Isn't that the lifeblood of politicians? But look closely at the new proposed giveaways—such as the silly notion, taken up by both presidential candidates for the 2024 campaign, of reducing taxes on people who get tips but not those who earn wages. The proposal primarily exacerbates the existing inequities in the tax code rather than addresses any fundamental problem.

> **Our government treats future generations as adolescents who cannot make decisions for themselves.**

The result is a shrinking "fiscal freedom" that hits younger generations the hardest. They're inheriting a government with its hands tied behind its back. Sure, Congress could expand social programs in the 1960s and 1970s or cut taxes in the early 2000s when annual deficits weren't so high, but it left the long-term budget problem for the future. However, the future has arrived, and the bill is due. Guess who's expected to pay it?

Our government treats future generations as adolescents who cannot make decisions for themselves. These politicians, akin to elderly individuals lacking faith in their offspring, entrust all their assets to trusts that dictate the precise allocation of funds and any interest accrued from them.

Beyond Zombie Rule

Headache #2: The "Political Prisoner's Dilemma"

I mentioned the Prisoner's Dilemma above. In an example from game theory, two captured suspects can either stay quiet or rat each other out. If they both stay silent, they get a light sentence. If one chooses to rat and the other remains silent, the individual who chooses to rat escapes, while the other receives a severe punishment. If they both rat, they both get medium sentences. The complication is that when acting alone, it always pays to rat. Try it.

The Prisoner's Dilemma

Pretend you're suspect 2 and don't know what suspect 1 says in the other room. If suspect 1 rats, so should you. And if suspect 1 doesn't rat, you should still rat.

Our budget mess is like that, but with politicians instead of prisoners. Both parties know we must address our fiscal problems, but neither wants to make the first move. Why? It's because they're afraid of losing the election.

Democrats remember losing control of Congress in 1994 after raising taxes. Republicans recall George H.W. Bush losing re-election in 1992 after breaking his "no new taxes" promise. They're both trapped in a time loop, reliving their worst political nightmares.

Beyond Zombie Rule

And it's true. If you lead, you often lose in the current setting. In classic game theory, the way out of a dilemma usually requires compromise, goodwill, trust, or constraints that "tie to the mast" both parties. As bad as a balanced budget rule was in times of recession, it was a mutually reinforcing rule that limited politicians' ability to give away the future. It was a bad short-term fiscal policy but a good long-term policy.

Meanwhile, we voters aren't helping. Polls show we don't want to give up on any promise for how much our future Social Security or Medicare benefits will be increased, though few under age 50 have any idea what that amount is. We definitely want to avoid paying higher taxes. We've gotten used to having ever more cake while eating it, too, so we're not keen on changing our diet.

Special interest groups make it even worse. Try to cut any veterans' benefits that treat Pentagon warriors the same as those who serve in theaters of war. Prepare for a media blitz that'll make you look like you hate America. Want to close a tax loophole? Get ready for an army of lobbyists to descend on Washington. Say you want a larger share of existing government spending for the young. Prepare to face accusations of inciting generational conflict.

It's gotten so bad that party leaders use committee assignments like carrots and sticks, rewarding ideological purity and punishing flexibility. The result? Government shutdown, threats to default on the national debt, and broadscale government dysfunction.

Beyond Zombie Rule

Headache #3: The "Can't Fix What's Already Broken" Blues

The twist to our story is that elected officials want to do stuff. They come to Washington with big ideas about improving education, strengthening national defense, fixing healthcare, cutting taxes, and much more. However, they swiftly discover that the promises made by their predecessors limit their options. An assessment made of Robert Moses, a powerful urban planner in New York City, is appropriate here: "He wanted to do good, but he wanted to do well first."

Right now, these officials have inherited a house where every room is already full of stuff, and they can't move anything out without someone throwing a fit. Want to fund a new program for those of working age? Sorry, that money's already been promised to retirees. Want to cut taxes to stimulate the economy? Oops, we're already running massive deficits.

The only way to make room for new priorities in this situation is to keep running massive deficits or break old promises. Examples include telling those retiring 20 years from now they can't have all the benefits they had previously been promised and informing taxpayers they'll have to pay more for what the government provides them.

Unfortunately, this problem has only worsened the longer we have waited to address it, as program outlays and interest costs swell automatically. Every year of delay adds to the size of the takeaways required of future legislators, as our existing obligations continue compounding faster than our revenues.

So, Where Does This Leave Us?

To be honest, our leaders are in a pretty tight spot. They're stuck between a rock and a hard place. They've learned that telling the truth about our fiscal problems is political suicide, but not fixing them is national suicide.

> **Most officials probably hate the pressure to vote only party-line and appear more as robots than independent thinkers.**

The three political headaches are complicated and interrelated, making them easy to demagogue and difficult to discuss politically. Try explaining the intricacies of Social Security funding in a 30-second campaign ad. Go ahead; I'll wait.

Our political landscape isn't helping, either. As political parties have weakened, special interest groups have stepped in, further incentivizing inaction. Gerrymandering has created more solidly "red" and "blue" districts, reducing the need for compromise.

The result? Hardliners on both sides increasingly dominate Congress, with moderates becoming as rare as bipartisan bill-signing ceremonies. Razor-thin margins decide many races today, with control of Congress and the presidency hanging in the balance.

Now, don't get me wrong. Many legislators I know are not pleased with this situation. But they are being elected into a system with these problems built in. Most officials probably hate the pressure to vote only party-line and appear more as robots than the independent thinkers they claim to be.

Looking Ahead: Can We Deal With This Mess?

We can fix this mess. However, it requires addressing not just the economic consequences of this failed system but also the political disorders that created it. Otherwise, even if some fairies magically put the budget on a sustainable path today, havoc would begin anew tomorrow.

For budget wonks, I'm simply suggesting something like the PAYGO rule that applied to new legislation (discussed in Chapter 4) be applied somehow to old spending and taxes as well—that is, to all spending increases and tax reductions, but over economic cycles.

Restoring fiscal freedom or democracy won't magically solve all our problems or make everyone in Washington sing "Kumbaya." This is a necessary first step if we want a government that can handle this decade's, next decade's, and future ones.

Resolving the Prisoner's Dilemma requires both parties' willingness to govern when elected—even when the language of elections

Beyond Zombie Rule

revolves not around governing but blaming, attacking, and making outrageous promises.

As for fixing what's already broken, we've done it before. This time around, reestablishing fiscal democracy sets the stage. Once a significant share of the new revenues from economic growth remains uncommitted, further compromise becomes much easier. In terms of giveaways and takeaways, Congress, with some fiscal freedom, can purchase reform through new net giveaways, compared to previous years' offerings.

Does anyone really think these political headaches are more challenging to treat than those facing the nation at its founding or during the Industrial Revolution? Sure, they're different. They're new. They require creativity. But harder? Give me a break.

So, next time you hear politicians promising more giveaways without mentioning the inevitable takeaways required or engaging in partisan warfare without resolving anything, ask them whether their economic promises make sense without treating these three political disorders. Ask them how we can start having the honest conversations required to create a government that works for all of us—not just for the ghosts of policies past.

In summary, three major political headaches hamper fiscal reform in the United States: the "Fiscal Freedom Nosedive," the "Political Prisoner's Dilemma," and the "Can't Fix What's Already Broken" Blues. These disorders result in a lack of

Beyond Zombie Rule

fiscal flexibility, a reluctance to make necessary changes due to political risks, and an inability to address current issues due to past commitments. The chapter argues that addressing these political disorders is crucial for meaningful fiscal reform and suggests that restoring fiscal freedom could pave the way for more effective governance.

We next turn attention to the counterrevolutionaries actively fighting against necessary change—the arguments and tactics used by those who benefit from the current system and resist reform. Understanding these opposing forces is crucial if we hope to overcome them and chart a path toward fiscal responsibility and sustainability.

Chapter 8: The Counterrevolution

"The only thing growing faster than our national debt is our optimism that someone else will figure out how to pay it off."
— Anonymous

Hey there, anyone who cares about government working well (I'm guessing you're one if you are reading this book). Recall how debt levels have skyrocketed under every 21st-century president so far. Hold onto your calculators. We're still stuck in this weird time warp where we can see all these shiny opportunities for a brighter future, but then our elected officials won't untangle the fiscal knots of the past to grab those opportunities.

The political parties collectively portray the government's long-term objective as spending ever larger portions of our national income on interest on the debt. Hmm, is this how Democrats get a larger government and Republicans a collapse of domestic policy?

Fiscal Chia Pet

At this point in our story, we've seen how this slow-motion train wreck has been decades in the making. Our dear politicians (bless their hearts) have been creating and expanding these permanent programs that grow automatically year after year. Think of them as fiscal Chia Pets—add water (or, in this case, time) and watch them grow! Meanwhile, they've been locking in tax rates too low to pay for all this stuff.

Hmm, is paying more interest how Democrats get a larger government and Republicans a collapse of domestic policy?

You might think, "Surely most of our elected officials by now would be ready to revolt and fix this, right?" Unfortunately, they are too scared of the counterrevolutionaries who have already stored up ammunition. Indeed, those who personally benefit from this financial system are not willing to surrender easily. They're digging in their heels harder than toddlers who don't want to leave the playground. Their arguments usually fall into three main categories:

1. "It's all about the size of government, stupid!"

2. "We must increase and never reduce the economic security and certainty promised to the American people, no matter what!"

3. "We can always reform later. Let's kick this can down the road some more!"

Let's break these arguments down.

Beyond Zombie Rule

1. The Size Obsession

Remember when President Obama said, "It's not about whether government is too big or small, but whether it works?" That's still true in 2024, maybe even more so. With resources tighter than a pair of jeans after Thanksgiving dinner, we need a government that works much smarter, whether it's bigger or smaller.

Think of the government as a child moving toward adulthood, and the economy as a family whose income grows over time. As the child matures, it demands an ever-larger share of the family's income for food and other necessities. Meanwhile, the family's income grows, allowing everyone to spend more. Now fully grown, the former child can still share in that income growth, but there's a limit on how much larger a share it can usefully and rightfully demand. The family wasn't wrong about how much it gave the child to date. It's simply that the now young adult's case for a still larger share of the pie depends upon current, not past, circumstances.

Here's a fun set of facts: in 1974, federal government debt hit its lowest point as a share of GDP since the World War II buildup. The government also ran roughly a balanced budget that year. From 1974 to 2023, the average citizen got more than twice as rich, and so did the government. Annual GDP per capita grew by 233 percent, federal revenues by 216 percent, and federal outlays by 291 percent.

While these figures again expose the large modern gap between spending and revenues, they also reveal that the growth in GDP, not

Beyond Zombie Rule

in the size of government, provided for most of the increase in outlays and receipts. Even if those receipts had been increased or decreased significantly, they would have supported substantial real government spending growth.

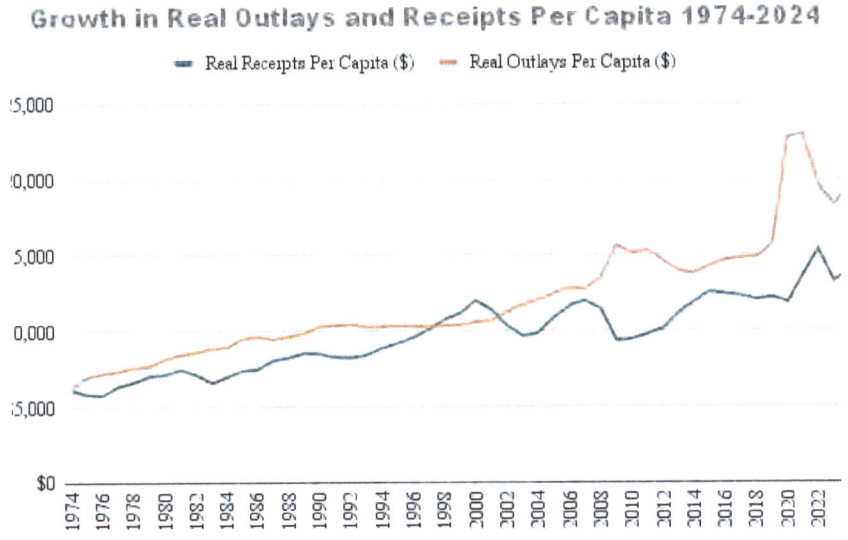

The same is true for the future. Almost no matter how we resolve the debt crisis and either downsize or upsize government relative to the private economy, succeeding generations are still likely to get much higher real federal outlays (and tax subsidies, as well as state and local outlays) than previous ones.

We've got one side screaming about the need for a leaner government while the other side pushes for expanded programs to address inequality, climate change, and the fallout from the AI revolution. Meanwhile, the real size of government, but not necessarily its size relative to the economy, keeps growing regardless of who's in power. It's like watching two people argue about whether to turn left or right when the road ahead can take them safely to their destination, and they need to agree on a reasonable speed. Like good driving, good government is the main issue for the journey.

> **There's a fine line between providing a safety net and wrapping favored groups in bubble wrap.**

---

2. The Security Blanket

Look, providing economic security is a noble goal. Heck, it's one of the reasons we have a government in the first place. However, the counterrevolutionaries are prepared to inform anyone who feels threatened by even the slightest change (tax increase or spending cut) about the harsh treatment they are receiving and the security they may lose. But there's a fine line between providing a safety net and wrapping favored groups in bubble wrap. Also, giveaways to some always have to be financed by takeaways from others.

Take Social Security, for example. It began as a way to keep old people from eating cat food during their twilight years and, in its initial expansions, provide a level of comfort in retirement. Now, it's supporting people mainly in good or excellent health for decades of retirement. In 2024, as life expectancy continues to

Beyond Zombie Rule

creep up through advances in medical technology (despite setbacks from the pandemic, opioids, and other "deaths of despair"), we're looking at supporting retirees even longer. It's possible and reasonable to provide certainty and security to retirees that their annual benefit will be more than sufficient to keep them well above

poverty levels and not decline as they age. It's impossible to provide future retirees with certainty that their benefits relative to their parents can grow forever faster than taxpayers' earnings.

Or, how about health care? We've created a system where advertisements try to convince us to tell our doctors, "Give me everything, and send the bill to Uncle Sam or some private insurance company!" With medical technology advancing at warp speed, it's time to ask this industry to start looking like almost all other growth industries, where relative prices fall, not rise, and a larger share of productive gains are shared with consumers.

Today, resources must be available to address new challenges from the gig economy, foreign threats, climate change, and many uncertainties we haven't even contemplated. When our government becomes overcommitted to increasing protections for risks identified and attended in the past, it simultaneously becomes ever less able to devote resources to address the curveballs the economy and the world throw at it. That's adding to risks, not reducing them.

3. The Procrastinator's Paradise

Ah, the "we can always fix it later" argument. It's the fiscal equivalent of "I'll start my diet on Monday." Guess what? Which Monday never gets specified. We have been making this argument for more than 40 years; during that time, we have become aware of the insufficient resources to address the long-term effects on the budget, such as the declining birth rate, the impending retirement of the baby boom, the escalating health costs, and the escalating interest costs that accompany each new unpaid tax cut.

In other words, the longer we wait, the more drastic the changes must be. If your debt is already at an all-time high and you continue to let your expenses far exceed your income, then every delay makes fixing the situation harder.

I discussed the need to be ready for new risks in a book I wrote on this topic in 2014, shortly after experiencing the unexpected financial market risks that led to the Great Recession. Within less than a decade, I had already failed to fully identify three of them.

(1) COVID-19 came along and said, "You think your budget was messed up before? Hold my beer." While much of the trillions spent on pandemic relief likely saved us from a deep recession, a significant portion led unnecessarily to increased inflation. In both cases, we never paid for any of it. ("Hello, future taxpayers.)

Beyond Zombie Rule

(2) Climate change went from "future problem" to "holy cow, it's happening right now." We're facing more frequent and severe natural disasters, which means more emergency spending. Guess who will pay the disaster bills for many threatened homes that can't get insurance? Mother Nature started charging us rent, and she's not accepting IOUs. The costs mount for both disaster relief and infrastructure upgrades to mitigate future damage. We're playing a costly game of whack-a-mole with hurricanes, wildfires, and floods.

(3) Artificial intelligence reveals how the tech revolution is moving faster than ever. Properly supported, it may help us reduce the costs of pandemics, global warming, and many other problems. At the same time, we can't simply address automation, crypto, cybersecurity, and a new future with rules from the past. It's like trying to use a flip phone to run Instagram. We already have AI systems that can pass the bar exam, write novels, and maybe even replace some white-collar jobs. Our tax and labor laws struggle to keep up. How do you tax a robot? Despite my optimism about the potential net gains to society from these developments, we must modify our education and social welfare programs to ensure their widespread distribution.

And let's not forget global tensions. From trade wars to actual wars, the world always provides new difficulties that must be limited or confronted. That means new ways to use defense, intelligence, aid, and diplomacy. It means preempting or addressing cyber warfare threats and securing supply chains for everything from computer chips to rare earth minerals. We're playing a global game of Risk but with real money and real consequences. And a budget that leaves no room to deal with any of this.

The evidence from history is quite clear. Our budget must be able to adapt to new crises. This chapter asks: How can we stop counterrevolutionaries from stalling reform?

First, stop obsessing about the size of government. While this is a legitimate issue, it pales in comparison to making government work better. It's not about how big the hammer is; it's about hitting the nail on the head. Today, this means leveraging technology to make government more efficient and responsive. Imagine if dealing with the IRS was as easy as ordering from Amazon!

The counterrevolutionaries have one big thing going against them: logic.

Second, rethink our approach to economic security. Part of this involves promoting upward mobility and helping more people build up their net worth in human and real capital rather than trying to catch everyone in one giant government net. Policies that promote saving, lifelong learning, and adaptability in the face of technological change require more attention. Attempts at progressive redistribution should be based on the means and needs of people today, rather than simply favoring the preferred clients of the past. For instance, let's eliminate poverty among the elderly—something easily accomplished with a modest fraction of the additional resources that will be devoted to future retirees overtime.

As for fixing things now, Ben Franklin's old maxim still stands: "Never leave that till tomorrow which you can [and definitely should] do today." Trees take time to grow and provide protection; the failure to plant them 20 years ago doesn't excuse the failure to plant them today.

Look, I know that making America fiscally responsible again (MAFRA), even if emblazoned on a black rather than a red hat, doesn't make for a great campaign slogan. But the counterrevolutionaries have one big thing going against them: logic. Their numbers don't balance or lead to the type of society and economy most people want. Something's got to give, and it would be nice to undertake reform that's timely, fair, and efficient at promoting upward mobility and growth, rather than a bunch of sloppy, unplanned responses to one emergency after another.

> In summary, powerful interest groups stand as counterrevolutionaries to fiscal reform. Their

Beyond Zombie Rule

arguments focus on the size of government, the need for economic security, and postponing necessary changes. This chapter finds these arguments disingenuous. It argues that we should focus on having a smart, effective government instead of worrying obsessively about how big it is. It also says that we need to rethink our approach to economic security because of changing demographics and financial realities, and it shows how delaying reform is becoming more expensive and dangerous. It concludes by calling for timely, fair, and efficient reform that better promotes upward mobility and growth.

Having examined the arguments against fiscal reform and how to counter them, we next turn attention to the practical steps we can take to move forward. We'll explore concrete ideas for creating a more sustainable and equitable fiscal future for America. We'll look at how we can invest in our children, reform our approach to retirement and healthcare, and create a tax system that's both fair and efficient.

Chapter 9: Stepping Outside the Hall of Fiscal Mirrors

Fiscal policy is the only place where 2 plus 2 equals 'we'll worry about that later.'

In our "Hall of Fiscal Mirrors," everything looks distorted, and nothing is as it seems. On one side, politicians promise the moon and stars without mentioning the astronomical price tag. On the other side, citizens demand top-notch services while clutching their wallets tighter than a squirrel does with their last acorn of autumn. It's a fiscal fantasy funhouse, folks!

But fear not. While it may be impossible to eliminate the Hall's distortions simply by adding new mirrors—like Congress does when it constantly adds new laws without ever reforming old ones—restoring a sense of reality requires merely stepping outside.

Possibilities that Fiscal Freedom Opens Up

So far, I laid out some rules required to restore some fiscal democracy. However, it's unlikely that the public would accept a reduction in excessive promises of high spending growth and low taxes unless elected officials can demonstrate that they are providing an improved alternative. Here, I want to sketch out a few things on which we can better spend our money—and even keep taxes at a reasonable level by reducing interest costs. Remember that the real tax rate equals the spending rate. When Congress

Beyond Zombie Rule

bills future taxpayers, government outlay costs don't go down simply because it borrows to cover them.

When Congress bills future taxpayers, government outlay costs don't go down simply because it borrows to cover them.

Let's consider some reforms across the life cycle, from young to old. A first step might be called imagining the "Kindergarten of Tomorrow." That's right, we're talking about investing again in tiny humans who are currently more concerned with finger painting than financial planning. However, if we pour some serious dough into educating these future leaders, innovators, and even TikTok influencers, we might avoid a future where "The Hunger Games" becomes a documentary.

Kindergarten of Tomorrow

Our success in becoming the wealthiest nation on earth in the mid-19th century was due in no small part to our emphasis on education for all, not just some aristocratic class. Later, programs like the GI Bill improved the

Beyond Zombie Rule

well-being of many veterans. Lately, our lack of progress on various educational fronts helped elected officials rationalize reducing the share of spending for education and related investments in the young in favor of ever more money for years of retirement.

More than just money is needed. We need to regularly measure each student's progress, not just attainment, and provide advocates and tutors as early in life as necessary so that each young person can better reach their maximum potential. We also need to rethink everything from the school day (sorry, farmers, but we don't require summers off anymore) to ways our schools prepare kids for tomorrow's jobs, not yesterday's factories.

As for workers, it's about time to attend to the future members of the working class who might not pursue higher education. This part of our society has felt neglected for some time—because it has been. The nation's agenda should prioritize work subsidies and ensuring that work pays better than welfare. Since most learning happens on the job, we should make much greater effort to offer apprenticeships.

On the other end of the age spectrum, we can do much better for our friends in the golden years. I've previously highlighted the ease with which a Social Security system, growing at a more reasonable and sustainable rate, can eliminate poverty among the elderly and improve the lives of most retired and disabled individuals with modest incomes. Private pension reform can also reorient tax subsidies more toward those with low and average incomes.

Beyond Zombie Rule

Meanwhile, these folks are like a secret weapon in our economic arsenal. Currently, we treat individuals who have decades of life ahead of them as disposable objects that quickly depreciate and lose their value. One of my retired Florida friends says they jokingly define themselves as PIPs—"previously important people." While many of these talented people succeed in finding ways to remain productive with families and nonprofit organizations, many don't, and that's not good either for them or us.

News flash: 60 is the new 50, not just for having fun but also for government policy. Sorry, folks, but you can't define yourself as "late middle-aged" in your 60s and then clamor for the government to continue defining you as eligible for "old age" benefits at age 62. It may be time for Old Age Insurance (OAI) in Social Security to be for the old.

Now, onto everyone's favorite topic: taxes! Our current tax system is like a game of Monopoly, where half the players use Monopoly money, and the other half use real cash. It's time to Marie Kondo this tax code. If a deduction doesn't spark joy (or, you know, actually serve a valid economic purpose),

Marie Kondo Organizing US Tax Code

it's time to thank it for its service and send it on its way.

This also means targeting the charitable deduction to favor additional giving, not those donations that would take place anyway;

Beyond Zombie Rule

orienting pension subsidies to better protect the middle class; and replacing subsidies for borrowing, such as the home mortgage interest deduction, with subsidies for first-time homebuyers. Simply put, if they are worthwhile, most tax subsidies have the potential to achieve more at a lower cost or significantly more at the current cost.

And don't even get me started on corporate taxes. Some megacorporations pay less in taxes than your average barista. It's like they're playing a game of fiscal hide-and-seek, and they've found the world's best hiding spot. It's time to yell, "Olly olly oxen free!" and make everyone pay their fair share. Because of the threat that corporate capital can easily be located anywhere, we need to support international efforts to set a minimum tax on these multinationals.

It's time to Marie Kondo this tax code.

Now, let's talk about the elephant in the room (or, should I say, the overweight healthcare system on the couch): medical costs. Our current system is like an all-you-can-eat buffet where someone else picks up the tab. Spoiler alert: that someone is us, the taxpayers.

We need to put health care—much of which is paid for through taxes, cutbacks in the non-health part of the budget, and borrowing from abroad—on a diet that doesn't cut off essential services. We need to focus on prevention (because an ounce of prevention is worth a pound of cure and often saves millions in medical bills).

How can we spend $35,000 in health costs per household and never pay more than $2,000, as politicians love to promise?

And here's a wild idea: what if we let people see how much healthcare costs, already over $35,000 per year per household? Remember those political ads that say no household should pay more than $2,000 in healthcare costs in a year? OK, here's a challenging math problem: how can we spend $35,000 per household and never pay more than $2,000? If you think you can answer that, you, too, should run for political office. I know, I know, it's crazy talk. But imagine if elected officials didn't hide behind such obfuscations as paying for Medicare through more than a dozen sources.

Unintended Consequences

Now, let's detour to the "Hall of Unintended Consequences." This is where well-meaning policies show how they've managed to mess things up royally. Take, for example, our current approach to means-tested and other benefits. It's like we've set up a series of

Beyond Zombie Rule

trap doors for poor people. "Oh, you got a job? WHOOPS! There go your food benefits!" "Oh, you saved some money? SURPRISE! No more housing assistance for you!" You what? You worked through high school and put money into a savings account? THANKS! Your educational assistance will be significantly reduced due to these savings.

The Game of Economic Jenga

Believe it or not, our current social welfare system for the non-elderly—at least if you exclude healthcare—is not that large a part of the budget. But it's built like a game of economic Jenga, with dozens of ill-coordinated programs. Especially for anyone with kids, work just a bit more or, heaven forbid, marry another low-income worker, and the whole tower of benefits comes crashing down.

Alternative Paths

But fear not, brave citizens! There is hope on the horizon. We can build a system that encourages people to work, save, and marry without fear of financial ruin.

I see two paths ahead. If we continue to dwell in our Halls of Fiscal Mirrors and Unintended Consequences, we may find ourselves

Beyond Zombie Rule

consuming a lot of ramen noodles and our children living in their parents' basements well into their 40s. Or we can step outside these Halls into the light of day and the possibility of a much more prosperous future.

The choice is ours. We can continue down this path of fiscal chaos, promising everything to everyone and hoping the math will somehow work out. (Spoiler alert: it won't.) Or we can make some changes and tighten our belts where needed, so we can run even faster very soon. But remember, we aren't doing this just to get our finances in order. We need to start investing in the things that matter for our future, where the long-term gains greatly exceed the short-run costs.

Folks, it's long past time to deal with this fiscal mess. I've only briefly sketched out some possibilities: invest in our children, create real opportunities for all workers to succeed, stop treating our seniors like they're ready for the glue factory, overhaul our tax system, and put our healthcare on a much-needed diet.

———

> *In summary, only a comprehensive overhaul of America's fiscal policies can help ensure a sustainable and prosperous future. These include increased strategic investment in education, particularly in early childhood and for those not going on to higher education; a shift from policies focused on mere adequacy to those promoting genuine economic opportunity and mobility; and a*

Beyond Zombie Rule

long-overdue rationalization of policies toward older Americans.

Of course, none of this is possible without restoring fiscal democracy, which requires reforming major programs for Social Security, healthcare, and taxation. Reforming them, in turn, means not just making them sustainable but adapting them to modern realities. These include recognizing the unmet potential of older workers and the gains possible through more efficient, targeted spending and tax subsidies.

Making these changes will be challenging politically. In the next chapter, we'll summarize what we learned to chart a path forward, restore fiscal freedom, and end the "zombie rule" under which the government dedicates itself to causes that lie increasingly in the past.

Chapter 10: Restoring Fiscal Freedom and Ending Zombie Rule (2025 and Beyond)

"Just because you've hit rock bottom doesn't mean you have to stay there." — Robert Downey Jr.

Folks, America's fiscal situation has gotten even crazier! We're still in a precarious situation, but now it feels like we're juggling flaming chainsaws!

Let's face it: America is at a fiscal turning point, no matter how much both political parties remain in denial. Social Security shortfalls? Check. Medicare shortfalls? Check. The end of more than four decades of falling interest rates and often negative borrowing costs? Check. National debt scheduled to rise substantially above any level ever seen in this country, even in World War II? Check. Lack of pay-for programs to address major crises? Check.

The signs aren't just clear anymore; they're flashing neon. And it's not just the threat of some financial crisis. We're squeezing out the ability to do almost anything new, whether for children, global warming, the working class, defense, or any new direction the public needs or wants to take.

No wonder voters give our elected officials such meager ratings. Congress then turns to fights over culture, over which it has little

Beyond Zombie Rule

control compared to spending and taxes, where the Constitution gives it enormous power. Should we be surprised that we have debt ceiling showdowns and such high levels of polarization? It's gone from bad to "Are we even living in the same reality?"

How did we get here? In some ways, it started with good or at least reasonable intentions. We wanted to create a safety net and lower some really high tax rates. But now? It's like both Democrats and Republicans are living in the past, ruled by decisions made by folks who are either dead or retired. Despite cutting back on the share of the budget for everything else that might benefit Americans in their working and child-rearing years, the Democrats want to add over a million dollars to the package of lifetime retirement benefits for a millennial couple relative to one who's retired today.

The Republicans, in turn, want to cut further corporate, estate, and individual income tax rates on capital income, even though, in most cases, those rates are half or less what they used to be.

If you follow the budget numbers over the past few decades, everything else has paled compared to those two agendas. The Trump and Biden presidencies kept us on that well-trodden path, and existing law schedules those two priorities to continue forever.

Both sides talk a big game about reducing the deficit, but they're missing the point. The deficit is just a symptom of a bigger problem. Both sides have succeeded in enacting extraordinary controls over what future government should look like. They're trying to micromanage our great-grandkids' lives even before they are born.

This mess makes it more difficult to deal with future economic downturns, national and international emergencies, the long-term care crisis that is yet to be addressed as the Baby Boomers and succeeding generations approach true old age, and any new needs that may arise. Worst of all, it's weakening our democracy and distracting us from incredible possibilities.

Both Republicans and Democrats are trying to micromanage our great-grandkids' lives even before they are born.

But the good news is that we've done this to ourselves. We've tied our shoelaces together and then wondered why we keep tripping.

A Unique Problem Requires a Unique Solution

Now, you might be thinking, "Isn't this just politicians being wasteful, like always?" Not quite. That danger has always existed and is unavoidable. However, this book has demonstrated four closely related ways in which this situation is unique in our history.

Beyond Zombie Rule

1. Our "fiscal democracy," measured by the share of revenues not yet committed, has been steadily declining into negative territory.

2. Our current policies and laws incorporate this long-term budget imbalance. Even if politicians never pass another law, we're still in trouble.

3. Our spending is already set to grow faster than our revenues and economy, and increasing interest costs compound this trend.

4. We're squeezing out core federal functions, cutting investments (especially for kids), adding to the squeeze by not paying for any emergencies, and failing to fund new opportunities.

This is uncharted territory. This disease, begun decades ago, spread rapidly with the Baby Boom retirement, the Great Recession, and COVID-19. Our nation has never dealt with this type of problem. Our usual way of dealing with deficits focuses on a short-term fix rather than major long-term course corrections.

One reason that even higher economic growth can no longer generate enough revenue to turn deficits into surpluses is that the largest unsustainable mandatory programs have been scheduled to grow even faster when the economy grows faster. Politicians can no longer easily collaborate to split up the goodies made possible by the rising revenues accompanying economic growth—because we've already promised all that money away!

Beyond Zombie Rule

Getting From a Vicious to a Virtuous Cycle

So, how do we fix this mess? We need to shift focus. Instead of just worrying about the size of government—that debate will never end—we need to rebalance our policies and adopt good government practices that would apply in Democratic and Republican governments alike. We must invest more in children, focus on creating opportunities for all Americans, and make government leaner and more efficient at working toward its goals. Adding to the population's human capital is one of the best ways to grow. Combined with a budget that leaves significant amounts of future resources uncommitted until that future arrives, it can convert our current vicious cycle into a virtuous one.

But how do we get from here to there? Will the right leaders magically appear and save us? Will a president and Congress suddenly rise above their partisan bickering, focus on the real challenges, restore fiscal freedom, and give current and future generations the power to set their own priorities? Many Americans hope so. But it's not that simple.

You see, elected officials work within a set of rules, processes, and institutions. Each has its own set of incentives—for more or less spending, higher or lower taxes, more or fewer permanent programs, balanced or unbalanced budgets, and so on. To make real progress, we need to reform these rules, processes, and institutions.

We need a "big fix"—a grand compromise between Democrats and Republicans. Each side must scale back its top priorities. To achieve

Beyond Zombie Rule

the greater good, they must escape their mutual Prisoner's Dilemma by tying themselves to the mast so that no Siren can lead

them, like Odysseus, to steer a course toward a fiscal shipwreck. This entails more than just reducing deficits and re-engaging some of the modestly successful budget agreements in the 1980s and early 1990s. It's about fundamentally changing how we approach fiscal policy.

What does history tell us how to do this? In previous fiscal turning points, policymakers pursued institutional reform when the math and new problems demanded it. They then succeeded because they created institutional structures adaptable to future needs and wants. They got out of their fiscal bind AND gave their successors the fiscal freedom to act. They didn't replace one rigid agenda with another.

Consider the period leading up to the formation of a new constitutional government. They figured out how to pay war debts, finance essential government functions and become creditworthy among other nations. But they didn't try to dictate exactly how the new central government would spend or raise revenue in the coming decades.

Or look at the Progressive Era. They made big changes, such as establishing an income tax, an antitrust policy, and a monetary authority. But they couldn't have known how these would evolve,

Beyond Zombie Rule

including how the income tax helped make possible our survival through two world wars.

These turning points were different, but they had three things in common:

1. They created greater fiscal freedom.
2. This new freedom opened new possibilities.
3. Leaders recognized that progress required fixing broken government institutions.

The solution to today's situation shares those common attributes. Obviously, we can't continue with a budget that forecloses future possibilities and a Congress that abandons its responsibilities. The only way out is a bipartisan agreement to restore a working order by sufficiently reducing past promises and, within our Madisonian system of checks and balances, convincing both Houses of Congress and the President to cease committing to any spending action not supportable by the existing tax structure.

So what institutional fixes are we talking about? Some want to amend the Constitution to require specific fiscal outcomes, like a balanced budget. Others suggest more modest changes to how agencies and programs operate.

But here's the thing: enshrining fiscal rules into the Constitution could easily lead to unintended consequences. The last thing you want is to put some economist's theory (maybe even mine) into the Constitution and have the Supreme Court interpret what it means. Plus, the government already is empowered to address this challenge. We need incentives and structures for current policymakers to exert less control over future policymakers and voters, including the debt they leave them.

That requires a true "grand compromise" between the two political parties, along with changes that make the budget process more transparent to average Americans. So, what might this "grand compromise" look like now that we're entering the second quarter of the 21st century?

Two Necessary Rules and the Accompanying Reforms

Restoring fiscal democracy requires two rules or practices:

1. Disallow most automatic growth in programs other than those over a short period of time.

2. Pay bills in a timely manner.

On the spending side, this compromise entails allowing future legislative sessions to determine the total amount of increase or decrease relative to existing levels, a process that now applies only to the shrinking part of the budget known as appropriations. That necessitates a lot of program-specific reform, particularly for many open-ended health programs that fail to operate within a budget, and where Congress has turned over to private sector actors the power to appropriate government healthcare spending. The principle would apply to retirement programs, too, which currently have automatic benefit growth built in line with wage

Beyond Zombie Rule

growth and longer lifespans—that is, faster than personal income growth and, further, in ways not supportable given current birth rates.

Limits on automatic growth say nothing about what future Congresses should spend. They merely broaden the scope of what future Congresses can accomplish, while imposing rational constraints on what the current Congress can dictate for the future. In the case of a healthcare program like Medicare, for instance, the two parties would still fight and amend the program as to what benefits to provide and whether to limit expenditures through price controls or caps on some premiums paid, as in Medicare Advantage. What Congress can't do is enact or continue programs that absorb revenues that aren't there.

Down and Out Santa Claus

Tax subsidies, too, would need to be subject to a rule of limited automatic growth. Furthermore, we must set current tax rates high enough to cover almost all of today's spending in non-recessionary times. We must also set them at a level that can cover over a reasonable period of time any deficit spending resulting from a recession,

Beyond Zombie Rule

emergency, or pseudo-emergency. Of course, the level of tax rate required depends upon the extent to which Congress attacks tax loopholes.

This set of rules applies to all spending and taxes, whether new or old. In contrast to the PAY-GO procedure, which was primarily applied in the 1990s to new legislation, these rules would apply to any increased spending or built-in escalator in current law. No more playing Santa when we can't afford it!

While rules like these would restore fiscal democracy, getting Congress to pass them requires tackling many significant budget issues, ranging from the design of Social Security to a slew of inefficient tax subsidies. As a result, I've tried to highlight how important it is for a reform agenda to show the public how the restoration of fiscal freedom opens up endless opportunities for real progress.

In the previous chapter, I laid out in brief some programmatic reforms in major budget programs. For instance, Social Security reform could aim to remove poverty among older people, even as it slowed the growth rate in benefits or raised taxes.

These reforms, as a political matter, provide ammunition against counterrevolutionaries who will try to convince people who benefit from the current system not to turn over any power to future generations. They will mistakenly argue that fiscal reform equates to austerity. If done well, it means greater democracy, lower interest costs, attention to groups largely left behind, higher economic growth, and a reduced probability of some fiscal calamity down the road.

True reform involves a debate about what government could and should do well. Simple deficit reduction mainly sinks into a debate about whose ox would be gored.

Making policymakers more accountable would also help generate support for the two rules of limited automatic growth and paying our bills in good times. More transparency would greatly support accountability. In particular, budget offices should show all sources of federal spending growth together, whether from automatically growing programs or new legislation. We could then hold the president and Congress responsible for all spending growth, regardless of whether it stems from new or past legislation. The healthcare debate would be more informative if it revealed what households are paying on average, even indirectly through taxes.

> **True reform involves a debate about what government should do well. Deficit reduction asks merely whose ox would be gored.**

Similarly, net tax cuts or spending increases should not only identify winners but also explicitly state that future taxpayers, not yet identified, must bear the net costs.

Beyond Zombie Rule

The payoff would be enormous. Fiscal freedom is liberating. It empowers our leaders and people to tackle challenges and imagine a brighter future. It frees us to dream again.

Fiscal freedom is liberating. It would empower our leaders and people to approach challenges and imagine a much brighter future.

So, America, what do you say? Are we ready to build a future that would make our predecessors and successors proud? After all, isn't that what America is all about?

About the Author

C. Eugene Steuerle

This is the point at which authors usually write about themselves in the third person. I'll be more personal.

I'm married to a lovely woman and have twenty fabulous children, stepchildren, and grandchildren, all of whom make my life exciting and worthwhile.

I've been lucky enough to found or co-found the Urban-Brookings Tax Policy Center, the Urban Institute's Center for Non-Profits and Philanthropy and a community foundation, ACT for Alexandria. I've served as a Deputy Assistant Secretary of the Treasury in charge of tax analysis and followed that up with 18 books and many other scribblings. Among my policy successes, I've been credited with leadership "without which" the most comprehensive income tax reform in the nation's history would not have occurred. I put forward the first modern proposal to establish a child tax credit for the National Commission on Children and instigated two other major expansions of tax benefits for children. Find more information at steuerle.org.

My blog can be found at governmentwedeserve.substack.com.

Related Zombie Videos

Zombie Rule: C-SPAN – AEI discussion on discussion fiscal policy and the federal budget, September 2024.

Facing the Future: A Fiscal Day of Reckoning, Concord Coalition, October 2023

Book Index

A

ACA tax, 36

AFDC, 28

Affordable Care Act (ACA), 36

American Dream, 29, 60

automation, 10, 64, 84

average life expectancies, 61-62

B

boomers, baby, 27, 35-36, 99

Bush, George W., 36

C

Churchill, Winston, 20

Concord Coalition, 110

Congress, 17-19, 28, 32-34, 37-39, 41, 43-45, 61-62, 68-70, 73-75, 88, 97, 101, 103-7

Congressional Budget Office (CBO), 45, 51, 56

Constitution, 67, 98, 103

COVID-19, 10, 57, 83, 100

COVID-19 pandemic, 26, 39, 58

C-SPAN, 110

D

debt, 3–4, 16, 18, 22–24, 30, 42, 45, 57–59, 63–64, 77, 83

debt-to-GDP ratio, 56

defense spending, 26, 33

deficits, 1, 3, 9, 20–22, 24, 26–27, 30, 36–37, 42, 45, 52, 98, 100

Democrats, 2, 9, 23, 27–28, 32, 36–38, 41, 70, 77–78, 98–99, 101

Donald Trump, 46–47

E

education, 4–5, 10, 20, 38, 41, 44, 49, 59, 84, 89–90, 95

entitlements, 2, 29–30, 45–46

F

Federalist Party, 16

fiscal democracy index, 3, 11

fiscal freedom, 2, 7, 69, 74–75, 96, 101–3, 106, 108

    restoring, 21, 76, 97

Fiscal Freedom Nosedive, 66, 75

fiscal policies, 12, 40–41, 64–65, 88, 95, 102, 110

fiscal reform, 16, 30, 75–76, 86–87, 106

G

GDP, 47–48, 57, 79

giveaways, 13–15, 20, 39, 54, 68, 75, 81

Great Depression, 24, 29, 41

Great Recession, 26, 36–38, 42, 58, 83, 100

H

Hamilton, Alexander, 16

Heller, Walter, 25

Hoover, Herbert, 55

I

interest costs, 18, 40, 47, 57

J

Jean-Claude Juncker, 53

Jefferson, Thomas, 16, 23

John Maynard Keynes, 24

Johnson, Lyndon, 32

K

Kamala Harris, 46–47

Kay, Rory, 43

Keynesian, 30

Keynesian economics, 22, 25

Kondo, Marie, 91–92

M

Madison, James, 23, 67

MAFRA (making America fiscally responsible again), 86

mandatory programs, 4, 40, 44, 47

Marshall, George C., 12

Medicaid, 2, 6, 32, 48–49, 62

medical technology, 82

Medicare, 2, 6, 27, 31, 33, 36, 44, 46–48, 93, 105

Medicare benefits, 46–47, 71

N

National Commission on Children, 109

O

Obama, 36

Obamacare, 49

Obama's presidency, 38

Old Age Insurance (OAI), 91

P

PAYGO, 38-39

PAYGO rule, 74

political parties, 11-12, 31, 41-42, 73, 77, 97, 104

Political Prisoner's Dilemma, 66, 75

President Carter, 34

President Kennedy, 25

President Obama, 79

Prisoner's Dilemma, 37, 70, 74

Progressive Era, 13, 17, 20, 102

R

Rabindranath Tagore, 31

raising taxes, 29, 33, 39, 70

Beyond Zombie Rule

Reagan, Ronald, 22

recessions, 25, 55, 58, 71, 83, 105

Republicans, 2, 5, 9, 23, 27–28, 32, 35–39, 77, 98–99, 101

retirees, 47–48, 53, 61, 72, 82

retirement, 5–6, 15, 27, 60, 81, 83, 87, 90

Roeper, Tim, 3

Roosevelt, Teddy, 17

S

Santa, 35–36

SNAP, 44

supply-side economics, 25

Supreme Court, 17, 103

T

tax breaks, 46, 49, 60

tax code, 63, 69, 91–92

tax rates, 8, 25–26, 39, 47, 78, 106

tax subsidies, 8, 44, 46, 80, 92, 96, 105

Tea Party, 37

U

Uncle Sam, 2, 32, 82

Urban-Brookings Tax Policy Center, 109

W

Wall Street Journal (WSJ), 26

Washington, George, 15

World War II, 18, 26, 31, 33, 41, 97

Y

Yogi Berra, 1

www.ingramcontent.com/pod-product-compliance
Lightning Source LLC
Chambersburg PA
CBHW050309230526
45471CB00005B/2092